G000255089

More Memories of Leicester

Part of the
Memories
series

The Publishers would like to thank the following companies for supporting the production of this book

Antone Displays

Arriva Fox County

Barlow Blinds

Albert Browne Limited

Caterpillar (UK) Limited

Cawrey Limited

James Coles & Sons (Nurseries) Limited

Crispin Adhesives

De Montfort University

Drivers Pickle & Vinegar

Everards Brewery

High Voltage Applications Limited

Jelson Limited

Leicester High School for Girls

Mutual Clothing & Supply Co Limited

Pick Everard

Shires Shopping Centre

EE Smith Contracts Limited

First published in Great Britain by True North Books Limited
Units 3 - 5 Heathfield Industrial Park
Elland West Yorkshire
HX5 9AE
Tel. 01422 377977

ISBN 1 903204 08 9

Text, design and origination by True North Books Limited
Printed and bound by The Amadeus Press Limited

More Memories of Leicester

Edited by Ken Wheatley

Leicester - a city of constant changes

Time passes and as the years go by, caught up in the present, we barely notice some of the changes in our lives and the developments in our environment as they gradually creep up on us - such is the nature of progress! It is only in moments of tranquillity, at special occasions, events and anniversaries, or perhaps the chance meeting with an old acquaintance or happening upon an old photograph, that the memory is jogged and we have the opportunity to reflect upon the past. Only then do we realise how far we have come and how vast the changes have been, even in our lifetime, to get there.

Leicester is a vibrant and thriving city with an equally rich and varied past. The streets of the city have been walked upon by many different generations of Leicester folk throughout the ages, each with their own story to tell. It is their different characters and natures that have each left their own imprint on the city and made it what it is today - a reflection of them.

From its origins as an Iron Age Settlement around the River Leir, afterwards called the Soar, to its development into a Roman garrison, its occupation by the Danes and its growth around the market in medieval times, Leicester has never stood still.

Much of the infrastructure we see today was developed whilst still a late Georgian town with a growing hosiery industry and increasing amounts of wealth. However, the 19th century and the development of Leicester's railway system saw the town progress in leaps and bounds. Many Victorian buildings and landmarks, such as the Town Hall and the Clock Tower, remain essential components of Leicester's character today.

Leicester has been a silent witness to its development but, despite many changes, there remain echoes and clues of the past at every step around the modern-day city. The old town was designated as a city in 1919. Since then its incessant evolution has continued, adapting to the changing needs of its inhabitants as they endured two world wars and a depression, as well as celebrating Civic Week, the Coronation and many other happy events. In more recent times, it has also adapted to the requirements of access to a motorway and the tranquillity of a pedestrianised city centre.

We are fortunate that the 20th century was so well documented. We hope that this collection of fascinating photographs provides a nostalgic look at the not too distant past, revealing in the process the changing cityscape and the many stories it has to tell. Whether of notable Leicester people, events, celebrations or how the city and its inhabitants have survived through difficult times, each tale is part of the city's rich tapestry.

We hope that you will enjoy reading More Memories of Leicester and that it will rekindle memories of the past that have helped to shape the present and will continue to have a bearing on Leicester's future.

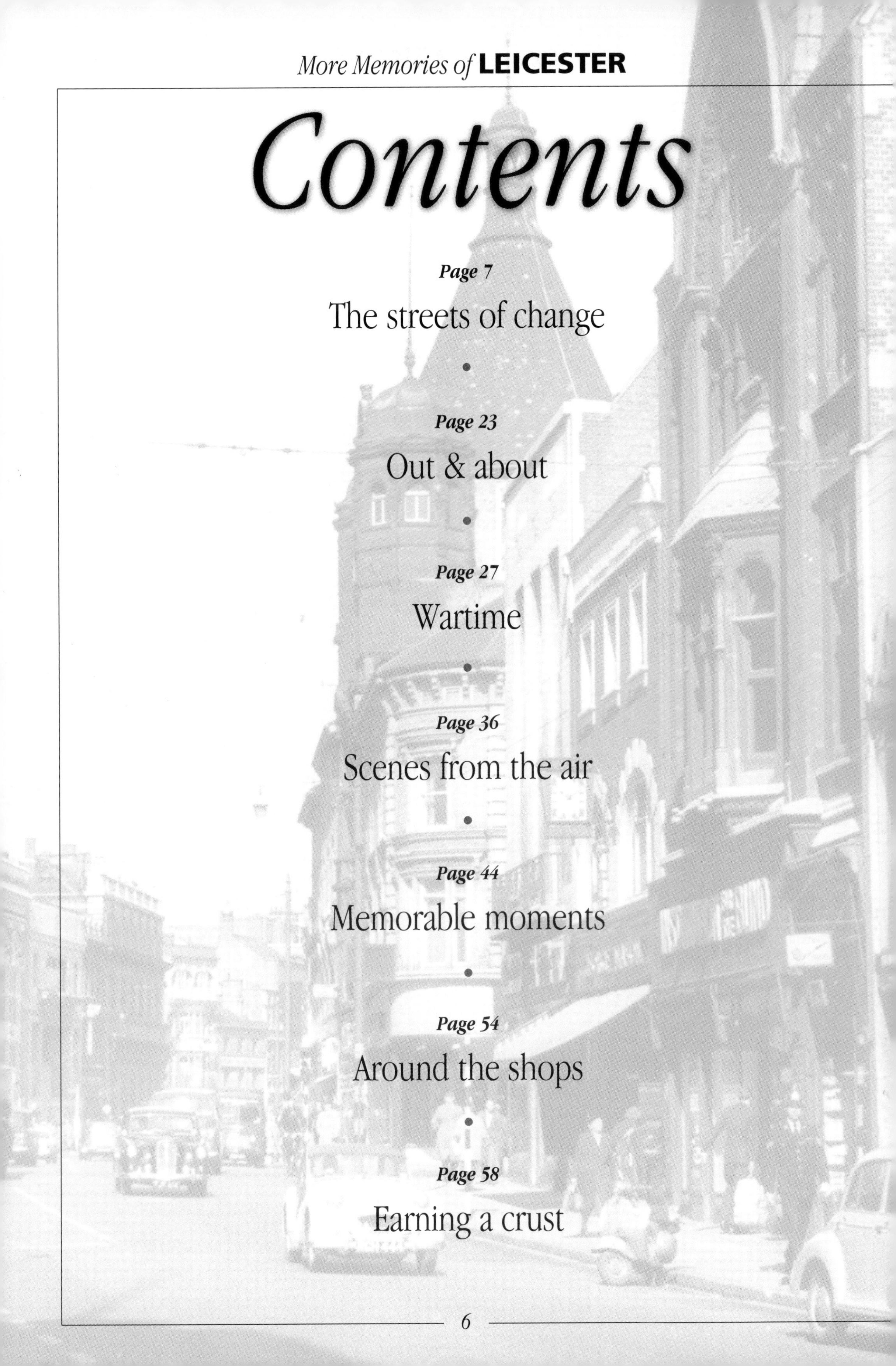

Contents

Page 7

The streets of change

•

Page 23

Out & about

•

Page 27

Wartime

•

Page 36

Scenes from the air

•

Page 44

Memorable moments

•

Page 54

Around the shops

•

Page 58

Earning a crust

The streets of change

To those readers who have visited or passed through the city of Leicester, this scene is probably instantly recognisable. Looking at the Clock Tower, synonymous with the city and one of its best-known landmarks, it may seem at a glance that time has stood still. However, with a closer look and to those readers who are local residents of Leicester, the Clock Tower which remains as steadfast as Leicester's motto, 'Semper Eadem', probably stands out less because of its constancy than the perpetually evolving scene that surrounds it. This nostalgic snap-shot of the busy bustle of activity around the Clock Tower in the 1950s hides within it another long-standing Leicester landmark - the Eastgates Coffee House which, in this scene is to the left of the Clock Tower and behind the facade of the Burton's store sign. The Coffee House was one of twelve such houses commissioned and owned by the Leicester Coffee and Cocoa House Company. This innocuous sounding organisation had in fact, serious and rather sober intentions. The company was part of the reforming Temperance Movement at large in the nonconformist city during the 1870s. It was established on a commercial basis with the aim to rescue working men from the temptation of the public house and its inexpensive liquor and did this by providing an alternative eating place where tea, coffee and non-alcoholic beverages could be enjoyed. The ornate building was completed in 1885 by the architect Edward Burgess and had an arched floor that was damaged by fire in 1974 but was restored to its full glory in 1996.

Above: This seemingly nostalgic view of the past, taken of the entrance to the Market Place from Horsefair Street in the 1960s is, in fact, not only a reflection of a time gone by but also an image of the present that will most probably be sustained into the future. Since the Middle Ages, Leicester has had a thriving market and the people of Leicester still enjoy the advantages of a flourishing Market Place today. The number and variety of markets once held in the town has gradually diminished but one popular market still bustling, shown in this photograph, is what was known at the time as 'Earl's Market'. Although more commonly known as the 'Saturday Market' the 'Earl's Market' can be traced back as far as 1298 and began in operation when it was given the authority to trade from a charter issued at that time. As the market developed, gaps in the ruined original town walls forming two sides of the Market Place were used to gain quick access to the stalls. Eventually, these alleyways, still known by the people of Leicester as 'jitties', became official rights of way. Over the centuries the market has been used for the sale of a variety of goods. Amongst these was the sale of corn from a wide pavement known as the Corn Wall. Cattle were sold at the Earl's Market until 1597 when a separate cattle market was established. Also, from the 16th to the beginning of the 19th century, the market contained an elm tree known as the 'Pigeon Tree' as pigeons were sold from under it for food.

Above right: Prominent amongst these hazy rooftops extending across Leicester's centre is another of the city's landmarks, the Corn Exchange. Like Leicester's most famous landmark the Clock Tower, the Corn Exchange can too, be picked out in this skyline due to its own rather less grand clock tower. Originally, the first building constructed on the site of the Corn Exchange in 1440 provided an indoor market for traders. Butchers and clothing dealers used the building at the expense of one and a half pence rent per stall.
However, the Corn Exchange that exists today was not completed until 1850. Before then, different buildings on the site were used as shops. In 1850 the existing structure was erected following a design by the architect, William Flint with loans provided by the Borough Improvements Act of 1846 and was used for the exchange and trade of grain. Six years later, it was decided to add another floor to the one-storey building and the architect, F W Ordish was employed to design the extension. A bridge was built at the front to act as an external staircase and, although this feature is now regarded as adding an Italian feel to the Market Place, at first it was nicknamed the 'bridge of sighs'! In contrast, the clock tower met with approval, as did the weather vane which was decorated with Leicester's crest of arms, the Wyvern.

Below centre: This mysterious photograph was taken in the 1920s as can probably be gleaned from a glance at the distinctive fashions worn by the woman in the background. Presumably, she was no relation to the little boy being led by the policeman. Whether the boy was being reprimanded for busking with the aid of his bagpipes or was receiving a helping hand is not known. However, what is certain is that this was all just part of a hard days work for the Leicester bobby.

Leicester's first borough police force was formed in 1836, before then, Ward Constables and Parish Watchmen had sufficed. The force consisted of one superintendent, five sergeants and 45 constables and was led by Frederick Goodyer who took up the position after leaving Sir Robert Peel's New Police Force in London.

Leicester's first police station was established in the Guildhall and Frederick Goodyear's family lived in the house in the courtyard. The prisoners were held in the three cells nearby which each, at times, was known to hold 17 prisoners. Guarding the cells was just one duty in the 14 to 16 hour working days accomplished by the first policemen who also managed to work 7 days a week and sleep in the roof space above the Mayor's Parlour! Despite this hard work however, it took some time to establish the public's trust and in the first year, 116 people were charged with assaulting the police and there were 15 rescue attempts to free people taken into custody!

Bottom: This Leicester policeman is hard at work completing one of his more mundane, yet essential responsibilities - that of point duty. It was not until 1929 that the first traffic lights were introduced to the streets of Leicester when they were put into use at the corner of Hinckley Road and Fosse Road. However, before the widespread installation of traffic lights and the advent of comprehensive road markings and signs, the task of controlling and directing the traffic and ensuring that pedestrians were able to cross busy roads safely fell quite literally into the hands of the police. Although by this photograph the police uniforms had evolved through several changes and no longer consisted of the tailcoat and top hat with the addition of the truncheon, the traditional blue colour remained. Point duty however, also necessitated the addition of white gloves.

One Leicester policeman who was regularly on duty in the vicinity of the Clock Tower was PC John William Stevens. Known as 'Tubby', PC Stevens was a well-known character, one of Leicester's favourite bobbies. During his lifetime 'Tubby' was Britain's heaviest policeman weighing in at 24 stones, three pounds and was said to be the inspiration for the 'Laughing Policeman' song. His popularity was such that a picture postcard was produced of him and when he died in 1908, over 10,000 people lined his funeral route.

Left: This aerial photograph provides a rare glimpse of the buildings to the right of the Town Hall, seen at the bottom left corner of the picture.
However, it was not until 1874 that the Town Hall could be seen at all as previously, Horsefair Street had been the site of a Cattle Market and the Guildhall was the seat of the borough council. With the population of Leicester rising rapidly, the demands of a developing town began to outgrow the confines of the Guildhall and by 1814, plans had been drawn for a new, larger building. Despite this and several subsequent plans of action, nothing was actually done until 1870 when it was declared by the Council that, 'Municipal Buildings were absolutely required for the convenient transaction of public business'. A competition was held for the design of the new buildings to be erected at Friar Lane. However, when the Cattle Market site became vacant it took priority. F J Hames was assigned the official architect and chose a controversial Queen Anne style in a time when the grandeur of Classical or Gothic styles was preferred.
The new Town Hall was completed in two years and on 3rd august 1874, the foundation stone was laid adjacent to a carving of a duck welcoming day and an owl depicting night! On the 7th August 1876, the Mayor declared the buildings open for public use and in celebration, a huge procession marched from the Guildhall to the Town Hall and a dinner was held at the Corn Exchange followed by fireworks and a Mayor's Ball.

Below: Judging from the rolled down shutters and the lack of activity, pedestrians and traffic, this peaceful view of the entrance to the Market Place must have been taken 'out of hours'. For if the once familiar clock face above Kemp's can be trusted, the time is five minutes to seven. Many readers will remember busier times when shoppers could stop at Finlay's tobacconists for a packet of State Express cigarettes before making their way to the Market Place. However, it was not until the 1970s that shoppers could wander round the Market Centre and also admire the statue of 'The High Cross'. Before 1973, the people of Leicester bought their fish from the Fish Market, a functional building with its roof supported by elegant cast iron columns. However, in this year, the City Council embarked upon the construction of an indoor extension to the existing Market Place and the old Fish Market was transferred to the new red brick building which provided more hygienic conditions for the sale of fish and meat. The Market Centre was opened in 1974 and the old Fish Market was converted into shops. One of Leicester's oldest markets, situated at the High Cross, occasionally known as the Townsmen's Market ran until 1884 when it was transferred to the 'Earl's Market'. However, in 1976, one of the pillars that used to support the domed shelter of the High Cross was planted in the current Market Place to serve as a reminder of Leicester's ancient market history.

FOSTER BROTHERS
FOSTER BROTHERS
LET
BURTON
DRESS YOU
WANDS
DRUG
Stores

From this impressive bird's eye view of part of the city centre the roads appear almost as extensions of the focal Clock Tower's hands. However they do, in fact, originate from a time long before the construction of the Clock Tower in 1868. In a clockwise direction from the top left, Church Gate, Haymarket, Humberstone Gate, Gallowtree Gate and High Street can be identified. 'Gate' derives from the Norse word 'gata' meaning street or road to, and of these road names, the ones containing the appendage 'Gate' can be traced back to the late 9th century when Leicester was occupied by the Danes. Indeed, this Danish influence even extended to shape the Leicester dialect still distinctive today. Humberstone Gate itself is littered with other distant reminders of bygone days. At the eastern end can be seen the old Victorian Weighbridge, now used as an office and the Regency red brick building known as Spa Place because it was situated on the site of a short-lived spa during the 18th century. However, Humberstone Gate was also well known for its May and Michaelmas fairs and it was at one of the Humberstone Gate fairs that one famous local was reputed to have gained his ugly appearance. It was said that Joseph Cary Merrick's mother was knocked down or frightened by an elephant at the fair whilst pregnant with him and as a result, Joseph developed a tiny lump on his lip when he was born, which developed down his body, affecting him severely, so much so that he became known as the now legendary Elephant Man.

Does this nostalgic view of High Street, taken from Carts Lane corner make you yearn for times gone by? The immediacy of the shot enables those readers whose memory does not stretch as far back as this era, to imagine stepping off the pavement into this bustling street scene. The large Magnet mounted on the corner of Whitcher & Co Ltd's shop front was once a familiar sight to shoppers in High Street. The Magnet proved to be a perfect advertising 'tool', even more effective than the traditional painted wall adverts that were introduced to Leicester by a Mr Fielding in 1866! Sadly, Whitcher's did not survive the changes in High Street. The building, however, along with the facade of the Co-operative Society now form part of the Shires shopping precinct. However, the building of the new Shires Centre, as well as replacing buildings from Leicester's past, also unearthed historic artefacts. During the extreme archaeological excavations, a Roman cellar, ancient rubbish pits, privies, cesspits and middens were brought to light, filling gaps in the area's past. When The Shires opened in 1991, the notoriously mixed fortunes of High Street were changed for the better and as the retail trade picked up, so did the interest in the area. The indoor shopping centre was designed by architects, Chapman Taylor and partners of London to incorporate the Edwardian feel of the High Street and in 1994, the centre was extended to Churchgate with a modern frontage.

Looking at this view of Granby Street taken from the corner of Belvoir Street, some readers will be reminded of long shopping days spent strolling the length of the street underneath the shop canopies. Under the canopies, engrossed in the task at hand it would have been easy to miss some of the magnificent buildings extending above the shop fronts. One such structure, prominent on the right of this photograph was designed by Edward Burgess and built in Queen Victoria's golden jubilee year, 1887. Consequently, it was named the Victoria Coffee House and run by the Coffee and Cocoa House Company who offered breakfast from 5 am, coffee for 1d and meals for 6d! Although no longer a coffee house, the building with its dome and ornate turrets, still proudly protrudes over the Granby Street skyline. From the corner of Granby Street and Belvoir Street can be seen another notable structure, the Grand Hotel. Several properties were cleared to make way for the hotel which was completed in 1898 to a design drawn up by Cecil Ogden. The Grand Hotel continues to welcome and accommodate visitors to Leicester in the same luxurious style established in the late 19th century.

Granby Street is also the home of arguably one of Leicester's finest buildings, now occupied by the HSBC Bank, but designed by Joseph Goddard as the headquarters for the Leicestershire Bank. Completed in 1874, the bank has a French pavilion roof, coloured glass and stone carvings by the sculptor who also worked on the Clock Tower, Samuel Barfield.

This page and overleaf: Both of these vibrant scenes from the 1960s highlight the importance of the Clock Tower as a solid anchor at the centre of Leicester's continual activity and progress. This however, has not always been the case. Before the construction of the Tower in 1868, the space it occupies had seen many changes. Records of the area can be traced back to 1260 when it was known as 'Berehill' and used as a site from which to sell agricultural products and hay and straw. By 1493 a pillory, cage and stocks had been added to the mound and the area began its life as a Leicester's Eastgates landmark. By the 1700s coal was sold from the site which changed the name to 'Coal Hill'. In 1750 John Bass erected an Assembly Room on the site which incorporated a temporary theatre and a machine for weighing coal brought into the town for sale. However, with the

opening of a new hotel at Hotel Street, the old building fell into ruin and functioned only as an obstruction to the smooth passage of traffic. Despite growing unrest the 'Haymarket Obstruction' was not demolished until 1862 when the site was levelled and paved. Although there was no longer an obstruction to the traffic flow the junction became a source of confusion and a danger to pedestrians, a few of whom did not escape without injury! Thus, a petition was sent round the public houses to lobby for the erection of a statue. John Burton, a local photographer who painted people 'by light', ran a studio near to the site and he and his friends raised the money for a tower to be built on the site. And so appeared the gothic square clock tower, 'to provide an island of sanctuary and security' and to show off to visitors at the Royal Agricultural Show held in Leicester in 1868.

From previous page: *Out of 105 designs the one submitted by Joseph Goddard of Henry Goddard and Son, Leicester was chosen and the foundation stone was laid at a ceremony on 16th March 1868. Only 12 weeks later the top stone was laid by the six year old son of the sculptor, Samuel Barfield and this time, after complaints in the local newspaper, a bottle containing different records of the event was also deposited. There was much debate over the naming of the Tower but in the end, 'Five Gates Cross' and 'Beneficent Place' were rejected in favour of the 'Clock Tower' dictated by popular custom. The visitors to the Royal Show had gone before the Tower was revealed in all its glory and the locals were left to inspect the sculptures on the Tower depicting Simon de Montfort, William Wyggeston, Sir Thomas White and Ald. Gabriel Newton as well as the controversial Croydon-made illuminated clock. Leicester had become the proud owner of one of the most attractive traffic island in Britain that was to remain Leicester's centrepiece for well over a century.*

Below: As pedestrians make their way along Granby Street, seen in the background of this photograph, amongst other familiar buildings, they pass the Grand Hotel with its elegant tower marking its location in the distant top right hand corner of the scene. After reaching the end of Granby Street, pedestrians make their way across the street, over the crossroads and into Gallowtree Gate with the help of the black and white striped traffic lights - a piece of nostalgia almost forgotten now we have become so used to the modern lights. Over the years Gallowtree Gate has witnessed many changes. Readers may remember Adderleys which, after becoming Marshall and Snelgroves was demolished and replaced by a typical 1960s construction. On the left of the street can be seen another, more enduring high street name, F W Woolworth and Co Ltd. As pedestrians make their way further up Gallowtree Gate, out of view in this picture, they would pass another, still famous high street name - Boots the Chemist, which was built on the site of what had formerly been the Three Crowns Inn. Finally, before reaching the Clock Tower end of Gallowtree Gate, there is yet more evidence of Leicester's rich architectural heritage. However, to see it one has to pass through The Angel Gateway into the Morley Arcade, so named after the two Morley haberdashery, fabric and curtain shops at the Cheapside end.

Bottom: Does this nostalgic view of Gallowtree Gate bring back fond memories of productive shopping days in Leicester? Perhaps you yourself were a part of another such busy scene in Gallowtree Gate or perhaps you can even spot yourself amongst the shoppers in this photograph. Whatever the case you, like these pedestrians, in their urgency to accomplish the list of tasks for the day, probably did not have time to stop and contemplate the rich and varied history of the street and the fate of those who have walked along it through the centuries. Whilst the shoppers in the photograph were free to browse round Hiltons shoe store and pop into Boots the Chemist for a prescription before enjoying one of Elizabeth's home made cakes, some of Leicester's residents before them were not so lucky. As the name suggests, in years gone by, Gallowtree Gate was part of the last journey for condemned criminals on their way to public execution. The street used to extend from where the Clock Tower is today to the present Victoria Park Gates and the gruesome gallows themselves were situated at the top of what is now London Road. Today, the people of Leicester prefer to mete out a different form of punishment by housing modern day criminals within the high walls of Leicester prison. Past residents of Gallowtree Gate have also showed their more community spirited side. In 1761 a group of residents clubbed together to buy and install some oil lamps in the street, to replace hand-held lanterns. These lamps were, in fact, the first streetlights in the town.

Shown here bathed in sunshine during the 1960s, Granby Street had experienced varying degrees of popularity throughout its existence. The street was given the name, Granby, after the Marquess of Granby (1721-1776) who, as well as being a professional soldier, owned land in the area and was the son of the Duke of Rutland. At one stage in its history, Granby Street was Leicester's main road to London and, as such, witnessed vast numbers of passing travellers to and from the capital. In this photograph however, and to an even greater extent today due to the control of through traffic in the city, Granby Street has become a more tranquil shopping street in which pedestrians can browse at a leisurely pace. Many extraordinary buildings of a range of architectural styles

remain in Granby Street. However, one such building lost forever to the street was the Temperance Hall. The hall was opened in 1853 and was owned by Thomas Cook, a great supporter of the Temperance Movement and its Victorian didactic assertions that working men should be God-fearing, sober and decent. Rather aptly then, the Temperance Hall became the first building to receive pure water from the Thornton Reservoir. That was not the building's only claim to fame. It also welcomed readers such as Charles Dickens and Mark Twain and famous musicians and singers such as Jenny Lind. Unlike the Hall, the building adjacent to it, the former Temperance Hotel run by Marianne Cook, Thomas's wife, can still be seen and admired in Granby Street today.

This scene looking north from Gallowtree Gate to the Clock Tower and the surrounding area is, in many ways, different to the view seen from the same vantage point today. Thankfully though, some of the upper floors of the buildings in the centre have been preserved and many of the familiar high street names still line the same roads. Also, despite threats to demolish the Clock Tower in the 1930s due to the obstruction it caused to the increasing traffic, and the plans to remove it to Victoria Park in the 1960s because it was felt to be out of keeping with its environment, it remains ever constant. It is, in fact, even more prominent after being cleaned and restored by Pick Everard in 1992. However, by the time this photograph was taken the cobbled streets had long been replaced and the once familiar coffee stall at the base of the Tower could no longer be seen. Today, the flashing lights of the well-loved Bovril advertisement that decorated the wall of the Scottish Legal Assurance Company have been removed and the site is now occupied by the Alliance and Leicester. This busy area seems a lot less chaotic now, mainly due to pedestrianisation and the surrounding one-way traffic system. In place of the cars circling the Tower and the zebra crossing seen in this view, is one of Leicester's finest shopping precincts with its benches, decorative plantings and even a new bronze sculpture commemorating Leicester's rugby, cricket and football teams. These changes are no doubt for the better but it is still nice to remember how it used to be in times now gone forever.

Out & about

A typical street scene, in which the women of the community were gathered around a street piano player, was taken in 1935. However, this photograph could have been taken in any working class street or community in Britain at that time. The piano was one of the few instruments that had filtered down through the affluent classes of society to become, in its upright form and evidently its portable form, commonplace throughout working class communities. Until 1929 and the advent of 'talkies' the piano was played in the cinema. Also, despite the first BBC radio broadcast on 15th November 1922, families still gathered around the piano in the evenings for a singsong. It was not until the 1950s and especially due to the televised Coronation of H M Queen Elizabeth II in 1953, that television sets became popular in many homes. In fact, many people purchased their first black and white set to watch the Coronation. Until then, other forms of entertainment had to be found to occupy hours of leisure which, in those days, were markedly less than we enjoy today. This photograph illustrates one of these alternative forms of entertainment. The street piano player probably lifted the spirits of these Leicester folk who had experienced the depression in world trade during the 1930s and its unemployment causing the period to be known as the 'Heartbreak Years'. Little did he know that just four years later his services would be in demand again to bring cheer throughout the war?

Above: 'Then trust me, there's nothing like drinking; So pleasant on this side the grave; It keeps the unhappy from thinking; And makes e'en the valiant more brave.' Charles Dibdin (1745-1814). These sentiments and the many other pleasures of drinking have, no doubt, been echoed and debated in thousands of inns and public houses throughout the ages. Not so by the Temperance Movement which, active in Leicester in the 1800s, began to tackle the problems of excess drinking. The Movement's claim that there were too many pubs, was even represented in Parliament! Consequently, during 1900 to 1910, 100 Leicester public houses lost their on-licence that allowed the sale of intoxicating liquor for consumption on the premises. This caused a backlash of opinion and before the 1906 General Election, pro-pub posters were scattered around the town. Despite this, the first world war brought tighter controls over licensing hours and contrary to Dibdin's belief that drink made the valiant more brave, it became an offence to 'make servicemen drunk whilst on defence duties'. Very few pubs were built during the war and this was also true of the second world war. The pub in the photograph, 'The Shoulder of Mutton', was the only brand new pub to be built in Leicester at this time. Located at Heyford Road on the Braunstone Estate, the pub, later renamed The Falcon, was tied to the Leicester Brewing and Malting Eagle Brewery. Sadly, during the late 1950s this, and other small breweries, were taken over by the six main breweries and more closures ensued.

Above right: The sight of the Leicester Theatre Royal shown here, was once a familiar one to Leicester folk as they walked down Horsefair Street. Sadly however, pedestrians strolling along the street today can no longer enjoy the same view. The Theatre Royal was demolished during the late 1950s and the site was redeveloped for offices. This was not the only theatre to be demolished on this plot of land. It was made possible to build the Theatre Royal only by the demolition of another theatre built in 1800. It was announced that in place of the 1800 theatre, 'will be erected one which will only prove an ornament to the town, but be far more convenient for the play-going public...'. The demolition went ahead and in 1836 a new theatre was built to a design by Samuel Beazley with a 41-foot long, 24 foot 6 inch wide stage. The theatre was known as New Theatre until in 1851 it was officially named the Theatre Royal. The first play performed at the theatre was Sheridan's 'The School for Scandal'. Unfortunately, some of the play's character names such as, Benjamin Backbite and Lady Sneerwell seemed apt, as the small theatre with its 1,300 seats and poor acoustics was severely criticised. Despite improvements to the theatre, Leicester, known unkindly as one of the three disastrous weeks in the theatre after Christmas and Holy Week, could not support the Theatre Royal. After playing host to repertory during the last few years of its existence, the theatre was sold for £50,000 and demolished.

Since 1882, those wanting to escape from the incessant pace and stresses of city life in Leicester have been able to take time out in the relaxing grounds of Abbey Park, seen here in this revealing bird's eye view. Abbey Park was the brain child not, as in many other cases, of a generous local benefactor, but of the Town Council itself. It was an undisputed fact that Leicester did not have enough recreational grounds. However, the opportunity to provide more only arose in 1878. It was in this year that the Council decided to undertake some flood prevention work on the River Soar. After this was completed, 66 acres of the nearby land was purchased and converted into a park following a design by Barron and Sons of Derby. Still on view today, is a plaque marking the opening of Abbey Park on 'Whit Monday the 29th of May 1882'. The opening ceremony was attended by the Prince and Princess of Wales who formed part of a procession through the town to the park. Once there, the Princess planted a tree using a silver spade and the Prince performed the ceremony. The walls around the park contain some of the earliest medieval brickwork in England and within their boundaries are pavilions, bridges, gardens, tennis courts, bowling greens and a lake. In 1925 the park was extended to include the Abbey Grounds and further additions followed including a Chinese Friendship Garden made in the Belgrave Community Workshops in 1987.

AF.S
M

Wartime

Both pictures: During the first world war, Germany had employed the sinister use of gas as part of its weaponry and at the advent of the second world war, there was no reason to believe that this tactic would not be relied upon again. Therefore, one of the all pervading fears, in the run up to the declaration of World War II, was that of a gas attack distributed from the air. As a precautionary act to protect citizens in the event of a gas attack, and partially to allay their fears and reassure them of their safety, millions of gas masks were manufactured before the hostilities got underway. Factories around the country halted the normal production lines to assist with the war work. The masks were then distributed throughout the country and offered to every citizen at risk. Several different types of masks were produced to match the needs of the prospective wearers. Aside from the regulation adult sized gas mask, smaller ones were produced for children. For young children who found the appearance of the mask disturbing and frightening, there was an alternative, more friendly looking 'Mickey Mouse' mask complete with ears and coloured either blue or red! Babies were provided with gas helmets with bellows attached to be pumped by an adult. Civil defence workers had modified masks with rubber earpieces, enabling the wearer to use the telephone, as well as heavy-duty masks with their own supply of oxygen. Once supplied with a mask, people were instructed on how to wear them and, although not compulsory under law, notices posted everywhere reminded people to carry their masks with them at all times. Some cinemas and theatres refused to admit people without a mask and many places of work held drills to test the speed and efficiency of fitting the masks in an emergency. The slogan, 'Hitler will send no warning - so always carry your gas mask' brought home the importance of always carrying a mask.

The first bomb fell on Britain between Dutton Bassett and Ullesthorpe at 1 am on the 25th June 1940 and the sight of the Luftwaffe above Leicestershire made real what, beforehand, had been hypothetical. Total War had arrived and all of a sudden, as in this photograph (left) where the residents of Jervis Street in Leicester undertake a Public gas Exercise, the importance of the gas mask and the steel helmet hit home and were more readily accepted as a part of everyday life. The sound of the large air raid siren installed at the tower of Lewis' store in Humberstone Gate became more familiar and by the time the photograph below had been taken on 2nd May 1942, Leicester had suffered one of its worst raids. Though gas had not been used and, in fact, was never used, the threat seemed somehow more imminent and exercises, like this one at the opening of the new ARP depots at Western Park and Rowley Fields demonstrating first aid and gas decontamination, continued right throughout the war.

Below centre: The second world war, more than the first, held a different and enhanced fear for the people of Britain - that of attack from the air. The threat of bombardment from the air was no longer unsubstantiated as, to a greater extent, it had been in the first world war. Knowledge of the German Luftwaffe was now widespread and preparations for the event of an air attack began to be made throughout the country as early as 1938. A designated number of cities throughout Britain were chosen to conduct a kind of dress rehearsal for an air invasion in the shape of a blackout exercise. Leicester was named as one of the designated cities and, on the 28th of January 1938, the citizens of Leicester practised the procedure for the event of an air raid blackout. Comprehensive precautions were taken including, the obscuring of place names and any other identifying marks that would help the enemy to define its location. This photograph, taken during the exercise, highlights just how thorough the mock air raid blackout was. This Leicester worker is busy disguising one of the bollards outside the Police Station with his tin of black paint. The Central Police Station in Northampton Square was obviously amongst one of the most important places in Leicester to protect, along with other public buildings such as the Town Hall and schools. Later, thousands of sandbags were also enlisted and piled along the windows and doors, to protect the Police Station from bomb blasts.

Bottom: Under Hitler, the German's began a full-scale invasion of Poland in the early hours of the 1st of September 1939. However, appeasement was still at the forefront of Chamberlain's mind and only when pressured by the country and Parliament did he eventually send an ultimatum to Germany. That final warning was ignored and so, at 11am on 3rd September 1939, Britain declared war on Germany. The imminence of this event was felt throughout the country even before the declaration, and towns and cities alike set about preparing their defences as well as their citizens for the inevitable war ahead. Leicester was no exception and this photograph, taken on the 7th February 1939, highlights the city's foresight. From this early stage the general public were inundated with appeals for their help and although still hoping for peace, many gave up their time to prepare for the worst. Conscription was not introduced until April 1939 but before then, everyone in Leicester, from the elderly to the young, both men and women, worked together collectively to protect their city. Here we see evidence of this as some of Leicester's women work hard for their country as Civil Defence Telephonists. The Women's Voluntary Service was founded in 1939 and throughout the war women carried out a multitude of vital tasks from providing hot tea, food and clothes to fundraising and assisting at the site of emergencies. The Services' work was recognised and paid tribute to in 1966 when the Queen added 'Royal' to its title.

At a quick glance the eye focuses on the cheerful man in the centre of this photograph raising his mug to the camera in high spirits. However, behind his smiles and the brave faces of the children surrounding him is a rather more sombre reason for their camaraderie. The year is 1940 and each one of these individuals is having to experience, in their different ways, the effect of the second world war and the changes it brought to their everyday lives. After the opening moves of the war there was a brief pause whilst both the French and Germans secured their respective defences: the Maginot and Siegfried Lines. This led to accusations in the American press that the hostilities amounted to nothing but a 'phoney war'! However, by the time this photograph was taken any claim of the war being phoney had been dispelled. Despite being in the midst of such uncertainty this, the worst of times, also brought out the best in people. Volunteers rallied round offering their help and services. This photograph shows just such altruism. The mobile canteen seen here was known as Mrs Bernaby's Canteen after the volunteer who ran it. Mobile canteens, usually staffed by members of the Women's Voluntary Service, became familiar sights around the country during the war. They carried out the valuable job of providing hot drinks and food to people who had lost all their possessions in air raids as well as providing sustenance to hard working Civil Defence Wardens.

This page and facing page top: These two photographs, both dating from the same day in 1940, show scenes of devastation inflicted by the German bombing raids on Leicester during the second world war. The majority of air attacks took place in 1940 and 1941. Whilst the Germans had the use of their Messerschmitt fighter planes, the British fought back with their equally impressive Spitfires and Hurricanes. The deadly German V-2s did not fall on Britain until 1944 but, by the cessation of hostilities, over 4,000 of those lethal, technologically advanced missiles had been launched at the allies. Luckily, Leicester did not have to suffer the terrible consequences of these weapons as, attacks dwindled during the German invasion of Russia, which required the majority of the Luftwaffe's strength. However, despite its assigned 'safe' status, Leicester proved a dangerous place to live during several periods throughout the war in which it sustained significant bomb damage. In 1940 Coventry and Birmingham received a crushing attack which, even their heavy defences could not prevent. During this attack, stray bombs over Leicester killed two people in the West End and damaged the city's Football and County Cricket Clubs. Sadly, the worst was yet to come and five nights later on the 19th November 1940, Leicester suffered its worst raid. The people of Leicester had to endure the prolonged fear of an eight hour and 17 minute continuous attack. This was not all, during this time a total of 108 people were killed and 203 more were injured. 60 of the fatal injuries took place in the Highfield area and in Rutland Street fire destroyed the Freeman, Hardy & Willis factory. Other businesses in Southampton Street and Dover Street were also gutted by fire. It was only the prompt action of the fire-watchers that prevented the Town Hall from burning down after a bomb fell through its roof and into the cellar without actually exploding, but starting a small fire. Both photographs seen here were taken on that fateful day, the date of which: 19th November 1940 was indelibly etched upon the memories of the surviving Leicester folk. Both scenes highlight why, in the aftermath of the attack, the raid became known as Leicester's 'mini-blitz' - the destruction was phenomenal.

From previous page: The photograph on the facing page is of one of the worst effected areas, Highfield Street, and shows the annihilation of the houses at numbers 28 to 32. Only eight months after this 'mini-blitz' the Highfield area endured another raid in which another person was killed and seven more were injured. It must have been a melancholy task; no doubt carried out by ARP Wardens and other volunteers, cleaning the vast amounts of rubble from these worst effected areas. The groups of men in the photographs seem to be contemplating where to start! Despite their losses, when peace was declared on May 8th 1945, the people of Leicester joined the celebrations and 10,000 of them gladly attended a special service of Thanksgiving held in the Town Hall Square, grateful that the ordeal was finally over.

Below: It was not until August 21st 1940 that Leicester experienced the horrors of an air raid. Unfortunately, the air raid siren did not sound until the damage had been done. The first eight bombs to fall on the city, although missing their Aylestone Road Gasworks target, managed to kill six people in Cavendish Road as well as injuring many others. The air attack was part of the Battle of Britain fought in the air between Goering's Luftwaffe and the Royal Air Force. Throughout the battle, 1,389 German planes were lost, compared to 792 British planes. Realising that defeat of the RAF was not possible, Hitler eventually called the invasion off. Apart from the heavy losses, the Battle of Britain had a positive outcome, as it became the first major turning point of the war proving that the Germans could be beaten. Churchill recognised the achievement but also the price paid to gain it and paid tribute to the British Fighter Pilots stating that, 'Never in the field of human conflict was so much owed by so many to so few'. As can be seen in this photograph, other parts of Leicester also received bomb damage and New Walk, shown here, was not lucky enough to escape unscathed. However thorough the preparations, no one was ever really ready for the devastating effect of an air raid and the people in this photograph look shell-shocked as they examine in disbelief the bomb damage. New Walk had not experienced such disruption since its construction in 1785 and hopefully, it and the people of Leicester will never have to witness such scenes again.

The very size of Victoria Park, with its large open spaces and uncluttered expanse, was what marked it out from other, more shaped and structured parks set out in the late 19th century. Its character had much to do with the fact that before being converted into a park in 1883, the site had been used as the town's racecourse. The nature of Victoria Park made it an ideal place to hold an event with great numbers of people, as in this case.

Taken on the 14th June 1942, this photograph allows those of us who were not there, to gain some idea of what it must have been like to be part of the United Nations Parade in Victoria Park. On the other hand,

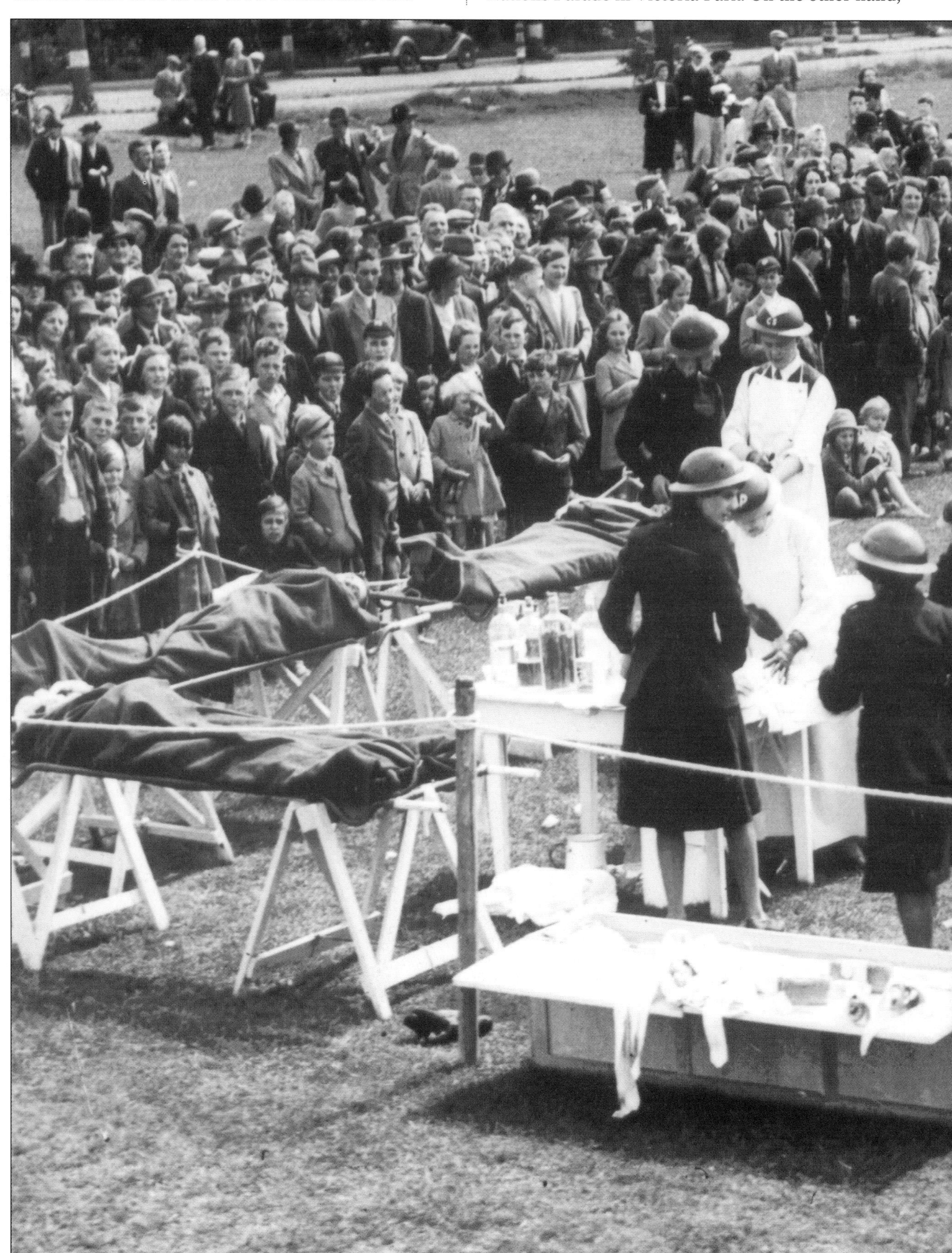

those of us that were there have the opportunity to reminisce and be taken back to that eventful day. Here can be seen just part of the huge crowds that must have gathered to witness the parade. The attention of these children and adults however, has been diverted away from the parade and they are engrossed in the demonstrations taking place at the Mobile First Aid Post. So they had to be as, during the war, more than at any other time, the probability of having to apply these skills was high. Also, just being in Victoria Park with its Memorial Arch designed by Sir Edwin Lutyens and dedicated to the people of Leicester killed during the first world war, was a sober reminder of the dangers they now faced from day to day.

Above: The second world war was different to the first world war in many ways. However, what was most noticeable by those experiencing it and, what defined it apart from the first world war, was its status as Total War. World War II was largely a battle fought on the home front, not only were servicemen called upon to do their duty abroad but those left behind in Britain were also relied upon to conduct their civilian duties. Leicester was no exception. However, in the classification of likelihood of being targeted for an air attack, it was designated an area of low risk and as such, was deemed much safer than many places in Britain. As a result, Leicester was able to welcome more evacuees than anywhere else in the country and 30,000 apprehensive people with their labelled belongings were sent to the city from London, Croydon and Ipswich. Due to its status as a safe area many of the restrictions enforced in other cities were not imposed on Leicester. Cinemas remained open and church services continued. Also, dim lights in the form of torches and cars with their headlights dimmed down, was permitted, allowing some kind of normality to be maintained even after dark! Despite this slightly more relaxed attitude, sensible precautions still had to be taken as can be seen in this photograph taken in 1939. Here, an Air Raid Precaution First Aid Exercise is underway and with the help of trained ARP Wardens, citizens of Leicester are practising bandage techniques and learning how to cope with the wounded in the event of an air attack.

Above right: Keeping the peace took on a completely different scale of meaning for local police forces throughout the country at the declaration of the second world war. Not only did the local bobby have to continue undertaking his normal law enforcing duties but also, the role was given extra gravity and importance during the hostilities. The Leicester police force was no exception and their solemn and serious faces, seen in this photograph, reveal their commitment and determination to the added responsibilities, not many of which were going to be too pleasant. This manifestation of solidarity and force did, no doubt, do much to reassure the Leicester folk lining the march that the police, wearing their steel helmets, were prepared to protect them against any criminal element be they German intruders or not. As well as the police force, the National Fire Service provided another additional protection for the people of Leicester. Fire Watching became a compulsory duty and all men aged between 16 and 60 had to organise fire-watching rotas. Later, all women aged between 20 and 45 joined them. The NFS took control of all civic fire brigades and worked to extinguish any fires before they could take hold. Whilst this protection was provided at home the Royal Leicestershire Regiment, The Tigers, were playing a brave and valiant role in the actual warfare around the world. The different Battalions fought at Dunkirk in 1940 and amongst many other battles, played their part in Crete, Syria, Malaya, North Africa, Italy and Greece.

Right: Only one person in this cheerful scene seems nonchalant about the procession - perhaps it was the dismal weather that caused the inattention of the pedestrian who appears to be rushing away despite the protection of an umbrella! Although the baby in the pram cannot be vouched for, everyone else seems engrossed in the event and cheerful in spite of the rain. These Leicester folk are, in fact, enthusiastically spending their time taking part in a Civil Defence Parade held at the beginning of the second world war in 1939. The procession, with its line of cars, cyclists and decorated trucks, paraded through the city in a show of solidarity. Parades like these were a common occurrence throughout the war years and could be seen in towns and cities across the country. Not only did they help to cheer people up and get them through the ups and downs of the war years, but they also boosted morale and patriotism, bringing people together and spreading the supportive atmosphere of a united front. Another collective activity, which had the same positive and optimistic effect, was that of fundraising. Throughout the war, themed 'weeks' were often held encouraging the public to raise funds for different causes. 1940 saw 'Weapon's Week', a fundraising week for warships followed in 1942 and 1943, and 1944 saw 'Wings for Victory' and 'Save the Soldier' fundraising events. No matter how small the contribution, just the act of taking part in a fundraising event left the participant feeling they had played their part in helping to win the war.

Below: Here we see yet another impressive procession, if a more formal section, of Leicester's Civil Defence Parade of 1939. Although civilians rather than a troop of servicemen, this does not seem to have deterred the onlooking schoolboys who appear interested in the parade and, in their naivety, are probably eager to become as grown up and important as these men. At the advent of hostilities thousands of men, unable to join the forces, volunteered their services to train and work as Air Raid Precaution Wardens. Initially, the Warden's main purpose was to give help and information to uncertain or worried civilians. However, when war broke Wardens became paid staff and as the war progressed so did their role in it. Amongst many other duties, Wardens dug trenches for air raid shelters, patrolled blackout areas, dealt with incendiaries, gave first aid to the injured and rescued victims from their demolished homes, cleared away rubble and supervised air raid drills. Their work was invaluable and sadly, many of the private citizens killed in the war were brave ARP Wardens. Working alongside the Wardens was another volunteer body: the Home Guard. Originally known as Local Defence Volunteers, this body of men also trained earnestly and worked equally hard to guard vulnerable points from possible German invasion. After several months the volunteers were given uniforms and weapons and, with their aid, set about bravely defending towns and cities by, amongst other things, manning anti-aircraft guns, communicating with regular troops and keeping watch.

Scenes from the air

This sprawling bird's eye view of the city of Leicester reveals several of its landmarks. However, hidden in and amongst the buildings that have grown up around it is, what was once one of Leicester's most important buildings, the Guildhall. The location of the Guildhall can be picked out in this photograph below the Cathedral in the bottom right hand corner. For many readers though, it is a building that they have grown up with and its distinctive timber-framed appearance is a memorable part of Leicester that seems always to have been there. The Guildhall dates back to the 14th century. During this period, a group of Leicester traders formed the Guild Merchant to regulate trade and industry and following their lead, several craft guilds and religious guilds were established. The most powerful religious guild was the Corpus Christi and it was for their meetings that the first part of the Guildhall was constructed in 1343. As membership grew the hall was extended and, by the early 16th century, with the dissolution of the guild, the Corporation had purchased the building for £25.15s.4d and put it into use as the Town Hall. Throughout its varied history the Guildhall has also been used as a judicial centre, a library, a college, the home of one of the oldest public libraries in the country, Leicester's first police force and a place of entertainment. Its restoration in the 1920s saw it being opened to the public and further restoration work in the 1990s ensured that it would take its place in the heritage of Leicester's future.

Seen from the above rooftops, Leicester's expansive cityscape is revealed. Several prominent landmarks stand out from the rest such as the Town Hall, seen in the top right hand corner of the photograph and to its left, the white canvas topped stalls of the Market Place. Further down from the Town Hall the two domed towers of the NatWest Bank loom over the area known as St Martin's. The bank is the largest surviving one in Leicester and was established in 1776 by the solicitor, Thomas Pares and his son after they purchased four acres of old Grey Friars' land. In 1900 the Pares Bank was replaced by the ornate structure now owned by NatWest. The line following down from the Town Hall to NatWest Bank

eventually reaches Leicester's Cathedral. St Martin's Church became the Cathedral Church in 1926 when the Leicester diocese was reformed; it was chosen over St Margaret's Church because of its status as the civic church. The Cathedral, originally a medieval structure, was heavily rebuilt in Victorian times and became the Cathedral Church in 1926. The shell of the building was remodelled and restored between 1844 and 1867 to a design by Raphael Brandon who added the 220-foot spire that can clearly be seen in this photograph. Later additions were also made by architects, G E Street and J C Pearson and, although life in Leicester no longer revolves around the Cathedral, it remains an important landmark in the city and part of its rich heritage.

Left: Looking down at Leicester from the skies gives even residents of the city a unique perspective of the area that cannot be obtained when in and amongst the buildings at street level. Two boundary roads, seen clearly from this angle section off this huge triangular area of the city. The two roads in question are Belgrave Gate and Humberstone Gate, coming together to form the point of the triangle. To the sadness and dismay of many elderly residents of the city, during the decade of the 1970s, a large number of the older properties within the confines of this triangle were demolished to make way for the implementation of an extensive redevelopment scheme. The nostalgic sight of the old tram sheds and their stables disappeared when they were demolished and several long established businesses and well loved public houses, such as the Stag and Pheasant, also disappeared forever. No longer could the old coaching inn, the Bell Hotel be enjoyed as a venue for meetings, special occasions and receptions. It was here that the meeting was held to begin the Leicester and Swannington Railway. More than that, the splendid balls that were held in the popular ballroom there became nothing more than distant echoes of the past in the memories of the dancers who had taken to the floor over the years. However, in place of these buildings was constructed the Haymarket Centre; the older of Leicester's two main shopping centres consisting of a two storey shopping plaza and a multi-storey car park. Also, in place of the old Palace Theatre came the now popular and successful Haymarket Theatre which was completed in 1973.

Below: The residents of these houses surrounding two sides of the football ground at Filbert Street would, no doubt, have an excellent view of one of Leicester's beloved sports - football. Football has been played in Leicester for centuries. However, the original game was not as structured as it is today and without set rules often led to violence. It was not until 1880 that several football clubs joined together to form the Leicestershire Football Club which organised both football and rugby matches played at Victoria Park and Belgrave Road. Four years later the soccer side of the club was able to break away and, with the support of the old Wyggestonians and members of the Emanuel Church Bible Class, set up a club of their own. The members each gave nine pence for a ball and the first fixture of the new Leicester Fosse Football Club was played against Syston Fosse. Throughout the first seven years of the club's existence only friendlies were played, but when the Football League was formed in 1888, it was time to get serious. The club began to play at Belgrave Road and Mill Lane and signed their first professional player, Harry Webb, from Stafford Rangers for 2s 6d per week! In 1892 the club moved to Filbert Street and was given membership of Division Two of the League in 1894. In 1919 Leicester Fosse was replaced by Leicester City Football Club which seven years later managed promotion to Division One for the first time.

This aerial shot provides a rare view, that can only be captured from this angle, of a wide-ranging vision of Leicester's meandering River Soar on the left, and its counterpart, the system of canals running parallel to it on the right. The River Soar played an integral part in the very development of Leicester itself and, whilst the city is full of historic buildings and landmarks, the Soar is certainly its oldest and founding feature. Over 2,000 years ago, the River Soar was home to a late Iron Age Settlement that existed on its eastern bank. The town gradually grew from there and it was the existence of the Soar that attracted the Romans to the site, who used it as a garrison before developing it into a middle-ranking

town. In 1776, the first part of the River Soar to be canalised stretched from the Trent to Loughborough. However, it was not until 1889-90 that the Leicester section of the river, known as the 'Mile Straight' was canalised. In the same year another West Bridge was built to a design by Borough Engineer, E C Mawby and, even today, remains the most important point of entry to the centre of Leicester. During the late 1970s the Riverside was transformed from its derelict state into an eight-mile stretch of footpaths and parkland also running along Union Canal which follows the line of the old Great Central Railway. This transformation was a large factor in Leicester being named the first 'Environment City'.

Memorable moments

Not just any occasion finds Leicester's Town Hall so crowded and neither does just any visitor receive such special treatment. However, the red carpet is rolled out in front of the Town Hall in this photograph in preparation for a royal visit. The flags are flying and the celebratory bunting is hung in decoration around the Town Hall Square which itself, is crammed full of on-lookers holding high their banners of welcome and eagerly awaiting the royal entourage.

Since the later 1800s the Town Hall has played host to many celebrations, events and important occasions. However, without the persistence of Alderman, later Sir Israel Hart, there might not have been a Square for crowds to congregate in. For, it was in 1879 that Alderman Hart presented the Council with a gift of the bronze fountain that can be seen amidst the crowds in this photograph. However, there was a condition, Alderman Hart insisted that the Council purchased the land surrounding the fountain and made it into a public garden. This happened and the fountain, along with the garden and its path, improved and re-opened in 1989, can still be enjoyed today.

Such scenes in the Town Hall Square were witnessed in 1919 when Leicester was honoured with its first official visit by a reigning monarch for almost 300 years when George V came to knight Ald. Jonathan North and as again in this picture, during a visit by George VI in 1946.

Above: By the time this photograph was taken in 1928 Leicester, like other cities and towns around the country, had survived through a decade, if not more, of turmoil. Though throughout the first world war Leicester had managed to escape unharmed with no bombs falling on the town, the cessation of hostilities had been closely followed by an outbreak of influenza which rapidly escalated into an epidemic killing 1,600 Leicester people. Housing was in short supply as were jobs. Throughout the remainder of the decade between 2,000 and 5,000 people remained unemployed. This depression was enhanced by the General Strike held in 1926. A day after the Strike was announced the Leicester Mercury printed a special emergency addition of its newspaper and by the following day over 12,000 people in Leicester had gone on strike. Eventually, the Strike was called off but the same social problems, although not as severe in Leicester as elsewhere, continued and for a time unemployment rose to over 9,000.
Two years later in an attempt to boost morale, the then Duke and Duchess of York, soon to be King George VI and Queen Elizabeth paid a royal visit to Leicester. Here we see the couple being greeted outside the Leicestershire Club in Newarke Street. The Duke and Duchess seem pleasantly amused. Not so the rest of the solemn Welcoming Committee behind them. Perhaps they were aware of the street's history, once called Hangman's Lane because of the public executions that took place at the nearby Magazine Gateway.

Below centre: Looking at this photograph, it is hard to imagine what on earth is going on! What is not hard to imagine however, is why the people of Leicester had turned out in their thousands to look up in wonder and marvel at the bizarre contraption towering above them - after all who wouldn't? However, the reason behind this congregation is revealed to those readers who did not actually witness the event when its location is recognised as Charles Street.
In the year 1932, it was decided to hold an impressive and spectacular pageant in Leicester of which the city's people could be proud. This photograph was taken at Charles Street on the 16th of June 1932, the first day of the pageant. To mark the beginning of the occasion, a suitably auspicious event was required and this was provided by the official opening of Charles Street. Originally, Charles Street, named after King Charles II, had been a narrow thoroughfare stretching from Humberstone Gate to Northampton Square. However, the street was widened into a dual carriageway and extended to Belgrave Gate. The new street nicknamed, 'Leicester's Million Pound Road' was expected to become the city's principle shopping street and therefore, its opening was an important occasion for Leicester folk. On his way to the pageant, the Lord Mayor of London stopped off at the Charles Street Arch lined all the way to the top with brave members of Leicester's Fire Brigades, and declared the street open. The rope, seen across the bottom of the arch in this picture was lowered and the festivities began.

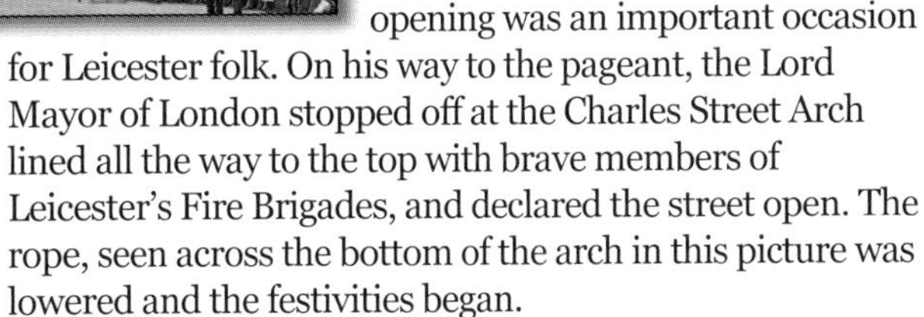

Left: This magnificent scene will no doubt, be indelibly imprinted on many reader's minds. Who could forget the memories of such a grand occasion with all its pomp and regalia? After living through years of depression this rare celebration, with its colour and wealth, produced many wide-eyed expressions on the faces of the children in the crowds as can be seen on the left of the photograph. This procession was part of an ambitious pageant organised specifically to boost morale and bring cheer to the people of Leicester. The pageant took a great deal of organisation but this paid off and events ran smoothly. The pageant had been advertised with posters on hoardings and walls around the city and gave Leicester residents something to look forward to, as well as something to enjoy and something to talk fondly about for weeks after the event.

The pageant was held from June 16th to June 25th 1932 and Abbey Park was the location of the festivities. Around the park, groups of actors performed the story of the city from the days of the Romans to the grand opening of Abbey Park. Scenes form 2,000 years of Leicester's past literally came to life as mock battles were fought and won. Longboats filled with Danes were even seen to sail up the River Soar in a re-enactment of the invasion of the old town. The fifth day of the pageant was designated Civic Day, a half-day holiday was announced and all the Lord Mayors in the country were invited to attend the event and process through the lavishly decorated and illuminated streets.

Below: In February 1952 King George VI was succeeded by his eldest daughter, Elizabeth. The nation genuinely mourned for King George when the announcement of his death was made. However, by that time his daughter was already popular with the public, as she had begun in training for the throne from a young age after being made heir presumptive in 1936 following Edward VIII's abdication. Also, at only 14 years of age she had spoken words of encouragement to the children of war torn Britain and from then on was taken to the nation's heart. This popularity was only heightened when, in 1947 Elizabeth married Prince Philip, the Duke of Edinburgh. Thus, on the news of the Coronation, the country rejoiced in anticipation of a new heir. Queen Elizabeth II was crowned so in Westminster Abbey on 2nd June 1953, a mere eight years after the end of the second world war and the country seized the opportunity to celebrate in style! This was certainly true of Leicester and amongst other things, the Humberstone Gate Fair was revived, there was a special civic service held in Town Hall Square, and the peal of church bells could be heard throughout the city. This photograph shows how, despite the cold and wet weather, the people of Leicester were determined to celebrate. Here, crowds joyfully line London Road and Highfield Street, the site of so much devastation during the war, cheerfully decorated in red, white and blue. As they watch the passing Coronation Parade, hopes are optimistically raised for a new Elizabethan Age.

Above: These were happy times for the people of Leicester who wholeheartedly joined in the nation wide celebrations to mark the Coronation of Queen Elizabeth II. Here we see just some of the children who chose to do their celebrating by holding a fancy dress party at Foresters Hall in Rosebery Avenue. The decade of the 1950s was one in which the country was beginning to emerge from the effects of war and start to prosper again. Morale boosting events were held in towns and cities across the country. Perhaps some of the children in this photograph had joined their parents and many other people of Leicester in paying the 19/11 for a cheap day return ticket from the London Road Station to St Pancras in 1951, to enjoy the celebrations at the Festival of Britain. In celebration of the centenary of Prince Albert's Great Exhibition, a government committee recommended that an international exhibition be held, 'to demonstrate to the world the recovery of the United Kingdom from the effects of war in the moral, cultural, spiritual, and material fields'. A toned down version of this plan became the national exhibition of the Festival of Britain held on the Southbank of the Thames near Waterloo. Despite criticisms of money wasting, the symbol of the festival, the Skylon was built beside the Dome of Discovery and 8.5 million people visited the Festival before it closed. New young designers were discovered and people were encouraged by the achievements the country still showed itself to be capable of.

Above right: It can be presumed from the plethora of aprons worn by the women in this picture that the photographer has interrupted vital preparations for the numerous parties being held for the Coronation in order to take this snap-shot. However, from the cheerful expressions on the women's faces, it does not seem that the disturbance was at all minded and, on the contrary, the spirit of the occasion is being embraced with party hats galore on display. One of the last times these women had celebrated a royal occasion was in 1946. It was in this year that King George VI and Queen Elizabeth had paid a visit to Leicester to offer their official thanks to the citizens of the city for the outstanding work they had undertaken for their country during the second world war. This included welcoming 30,000 evacuees to the city. The people of Leicester gathered in Victoria Park in their thousands to catch a glimpse of the royal couple who were welcomed to the city by the Mayor and Mayoress of Leicester. After seeing George VI and his wife, many felt affection for the couple and when the announcement of the King's death was made in 1952, the people of Leicester were genuinely upset. Although tinged with sadness, the Coronation of the new Queen was a joyful occasion and one that was celebrated extensively throughout the city. When the new Queen Elizabeth II visited Leicester in 1958, crowds gathered to give her as warm a welcome as they had done her father.

Right: 'God Save Our Queen May She Reign In Peace', these were poignant words in light of the turbulent times the nation and the people of Leicester had lived through over the four decades previous to 1953. Although still only schoolchildren in this photograph, the girls holding the banner would be well aware of the events and effects of the second world war, still present in the collective consciousness. The costume worn by the girl on the left hand side of the picture illustrates just how far reaching the effects of the war still were. The Coronation brought a feeling of optimism and hope towards the future, which included the keenly felt wish to see the end of rationing as called for on the girl's hat which pronounces, 'Off the Ration'! Bread had not gone on ration until 1946. Clothes rationing did not end until 1949 and petrol rationing not until 1950. By the year of the Coronation people were fed up with making a little go a long way, following recipes for plain dishes such as oatmeal sausages and eggless cake. Despite the continuance of rationing, the children of Leicester did not go without party food on Coronation Day. The Food Office produced an allowance for 100 children of one pound of cooking fat and four pounds of sugar. Also, to their delight, sweet rationing ended in 1953. The icing on the cake came in 1954 when rationing ended and people could finally tear up their ration books and, with the introduction of the Welfare State, look forward to a brighter future.

Below: Here we see more celebrations in Leicester at the time of the Coronation. A fancy dress party allows the children of the city to play their role in the festivities. It is hard to say which elaborate costume would have won the competition, but there is no doubt that the old fashioned black and white striped traffic light would have won the prize for originality! For many readers who were children at the time of the Coronation in 1953, this photograph will bring back memories of patriotic street parties, fancy dress parades, or just waving a paper Union Jack flag whilst enjoying an abundance of cake and jelly! As well as taking part in their own celebrations, many Leicester folk took a break from the festivities to actually watch the crowning of the Queen on television. The BBC network had reached Leicester in December 1949. However, the early sets were expensive and only a select few could afford one. The Festival of Britain was broadcast on the television and was one of the first times many went out of their way to watch the television, attracting approximately two million viewers. However, when news spread that the Coronation was to be broadcast for television many more people purchased their first set. Those who were not so fortunate as to own their own set, gathered around neighbours screens to view the special occasion. Another alternative was to watch the ceremony on TV screens installed in Leicester cinemas, the YMCA and the Co-op Hall.

On the move

Bottom: By the late 19th century it had become apparent that Leicester needed a new mainline railway station to cope with the increasing amount of traffic causing problems for the existing system. However, without the co-operation of the Midland Company it was left to Sir Edward Watkin to build the Great Central Railway. Dwellings were cleared, occupants re-housed and Great Central Street itself was constructed to accommodate the elevated station. After several delays the line opened in 1899. The impressive facade, as seen in this photograph, was ornate and consisted of nine Dutch gables made from Yorkshire stone with a prominent clock tower resting between them. The southern end of the frontage was dominated by a separate gateway announcing the entrance to the Parcels Office in Hathern buff terracotta lettering. Out of view in this picture, hidden behind the facade, were a booking hall and a dining room which in its time was thought to be second best only to Leicester's Grand Hotel. Once passengers had made their way past the ticket collectors they reached the quarter mile long platforms and from there enjoyed advantageous views of Leicestershire. Seen here in 1925, the station is thriving. However, its story is one tinged with sadness as, although built to last for centuries, it was eventually closed in 1969 after a gradual running down of services. Two years later the platforms and substantial buildings were demolished and today, only the name remains, as Great Central Way is now a cycle and walkway.

Right: Perhaps this 1930s scene of a bustling, action-packed Gallowtree Gate will stir in some readers, memories long forgotten since the pedestrianisation of the area and act as a fond reminder of the days when tramcars played a vital role in the life of the city. The immutable nature of a photograph however, belies the reality of change just around the corner. Three years before this picture was taken, the last tramway in Leicester had already been built and although by 1930 the fleet was still in excellent condition, the future of the tramcar was beginning to be questioned. Conversely, the electric tramcars in this photograph had themselves replaced horse cars which had been out of use since 1904. It was in 1863 that the first horse bus service was introduced to Leicester by Solomon Andrews whose apt motto was, 'Keep Moving'! In 1874 the Leicester Tramways Company was formed and its first tramcar operated from the Clock Tower to the Folly Inn on Christmas Eve that year. The first cars were all single-deck, one-horse vehicles, later improved with the addition of another deck and top covers. By 1886 the grey and biscuit coloured fleet had reached its peak with 46 trams in operation. However, the purchase in 1901 of the company by Leicester Corporation signalled the beginning of the end for the horse tramcar.

For years, before the pedestrianisation of the area, the sight of cars and buses circling the Clock Tower as part of their route through the city was a familiar one to the people of Leicester. The introduction of the motor bus had, in fact, been accomplished during the period when tramcars were still the prevailing mode of transport in Leicester. In 1913 plans were made to extend the tramways but the advent of the first world war meant that most of these plans had to be shelved. This set back to the tram however, opened up new opportunities for the accession of the motor bus. In 1924 the first motor bus route was inaugurated to serve the areas outlined in the abandoned 1913 plans and over the following years the motor bus fleet grew. In 1938, on the recommendation of the manager, Ben England, it was accepted that diesel buses should replace the trams. Although the conversion programme was delayed by the onset of war, in 1946 work forged ahead again and over the following five years 199 motor buses appeared on the streets of the city. The rise in private ownership of cars during the 1960s saw the use of public transport decline and with it, the number of buses in the Leicester fleet. Despite this, developments were made and with the addition of VHF radios and closed circuit television cameras the efficiency of the service improved. The last rear entrance bus ran in 1982 and since then passengers have been carried around Leicester in modern single and double-deck buses.

We are so used to today's sleek looking, aerodynamic cars that the sight of these rather robust, sturdy and square looking vehicles will probably bring memories flooding back for many readers who remember these lively and hectic days in Leicester's centre during the 1960s. These were the days before the pedestrianisation of the centre when cars, lorries, bicycles and motorcycles were allowed unrestricted access to the area around the Clock Tower. Much has changed now and no longer is there a need for policemen on point duty to protect and guide pedestrians from the traffic coming at them from every direction. Today, those people on foot are given the priority over traffic in the city centre's streets. However, this is only possible because of the development of a network of roads

serving the city and its surrounding areas. It was throughout the decade of the 1960s that a lot of the extensive road building in Leicester was undertaken. One of the most significant developments that we take for granted in our day-to-day lives now, was the construction of the M1 motorway. The motorway was opened through Leicestershire in stages during 1965 and almost immediately the weight of some of the city's traffic problems was lifted as the centre's through traffic rapidly reduced. However, the popularity of the motorway meant that approach roads were becoming more and more congested. Another solution was needed and came in the form of a £2 million investment. A central ring road was built between the Newarkes and Belgrave Road and in 1968 an underpass was also opened.

Around the shops

The sun is shining on Leicester's Woolworth store in Gallowtree Gate in this photograph and not just in a literal sense. The shop is a hive of activity with customers congregating around the packed window displays and milling in and out of the store, eager to spend their 6d! The fine weather has also brought many customers out into the city centre on their bicycles and, judging from the number of cycles propped up against the kerb, many had decided to stop off at Woolworth's. Perhaps they needed an item sold there or perhaps, they stopped for a well-earned cup of tea and refreshment in the cafeteria on the store's second floor. Some of the bicycles may even have been purchased from another, now famous, high street store in Leicester. Curry's Cycle store could be found situated at Leicester's Haymarket from 1902. From there, the Curry family began making and selling cycles and today, Curry's still has a shop in the city but it has now grown and evolved into a national electrical goods chain! F W Woolworth & Co Ltd, on the other hand, has remained in the same line of goods since its foundation. The British 3d and 6d Woolworth stores were direct replicas of the original 5 and 10 cent stores that spread in a chain across America at the end of the 19th century. In 1879, F W Woolworth opened his first store selling a range of goods at fixed low prices and by 1911, he had over 1,000 shops all over the USA.

Little would one know, looking at this delightful nostalgic scene, that there had been a specific purpose in capturing the city centre at its best? However, printed on the back of the photograph is a statement revealing the intentions behind the display and distribution of the picture - propaganda! The postcard was produced in order to promote the election of members of the City Council in the hope that voters would turn out in force at the polling booths on 1st November 1930 to make their opinion count. The statement is tainted with language to reprimand and shame the reader. After being told how proud the citizens of Leicester should be of their city, 'one of the cleanest and most progressive cities in the country', the reader is told how lucky he is to live there, 'its citizens enjoy probably proportionately more of the amenities ... than the dwellers in any of England's other municipalities'. The blow is then dealt that few of Leicester's 'inhabitants take the slightest interest in municipal affairs', that last years voting figures were very poor compared with other cities and finally that, 'This is not a record to be proud of'! By this stage of the rhetoric the reader is no doubt supposed to be wracked with a feeling of guilt which, the dogmatic statement suggests, can only be lifted by casting a vote, 'In this way you will show yourselves real citizens of the finest city in the country'!

Above: The modest sign, seen on the left, advertising Cook's World Travel Service does not seem fitting in relation to the size of Thomas Cook's achievements. Now a world famous name, Thomas Cook began his business in Leicester. At a Temperance Meeting in the town Thomas had the idea to hire a train and run a trip from Leicester to a Temperance Rally in Loughborough. In 1841, 570 passengers paid one shilling for the all-inclusive excursion and its resounding success marked the beginning of what was to become a world-wide travel agency.
Although no longer the site of Thomas Cook's offices, the frieze with its plaques on the upper first floor level of the building in Gallowtree Gate completed two years after his death, still remains. The first plaque dated 1841 marks the year of the first Cook Tour. The second plaque is dated 1851, the year of the great Exhibition in London to which Cook's firm organised trips for 165,000 people from around the country. By the date on the third plaque, 1884, the company was organising holidays around the world and in this year, was also commissioned by the British government to take an expeditionary force and their 100,000 tons of supplies up the Nile. The fourth and final plaque bears the landmark date, 1891 - the Golden Jubilee of Thomas Cook and Sons. Sadly, a year later, Thomas died but the company he founded continues to thrive in his name. Such was the importance of Thomas Cook's contribution to Leicester that a statue of him by James Butler was erected at the corner of Station Street and London Road.

Above right: Although this scene contains many familiar high street names such as Burton, British Home Stores and Philips, typical of many rows of shops in almost any city or large town in the country, it cannot be mistaken for any other place than Leicester. Not only does the unique Clock Tower indicate its location but also, the historic character of the upper levels of the buildings and their distinguished architecture marks them out from other town centre streets. The street in question, with only part of its long dimension visible in this photograph, is High Street which once contained the East Gate and West Bridge of the Roman town at each end. Today, the shop fronts display different names including Laura Ashley and McDonalds however, the upper levels of the buildings remain largely unaltered. Not so the road in the foreground which is now pedestrianised and no place for a learner driver as in this picture where the unusually quiet road affords a perfect place to practise. Let's hope that whatever diverted the policeman's attention in High Street did not distract him from safely directing the learner driver on his way! Although on point duty in this scene, with the advent of traffic lights, Leicester policemen were soon free to tackle the more demanding of their duties. However, aspects of traffic control not executed by traffic lights still needed to be implemented. So, in 1961, Leicester became the first city outside of London to have Traffic Warden Supervisors taking control of the traffic under the guidance of the Chief Constable, Sir Robert Mark.

Below: This rather subdued scene shows a handful of pedestrians dotted along Granby Street. Once the main road from Leicester to London, Granby Street gradually modified into a competitive row of banks and businesses serving the town's wealthy industrialists and then finally, into a quiet shopping street.
Although containing its fair share of fine buildings in various architectural styles constructed in the Victorian era, the street also contains many plain but practical commercial buildings constructed during the inter-war years. Here can be seen a selection of stores whose once well known names serve as a reminder of a time gone by. On the left hand side of the picture, Clifton Gowns, 'Leicester's foremost inexpensive fashion house' invites shoppers to inspect its new display of bargain priced goods. Next door to Clifton Gowns is Rivoli of Regent Street where shoppers could purchase a pair of Dents gloves for 2/11 before walking on to Sands the millinery specialists. Finally, the last shop in this row is Rational Tailoring which proudly advertises its claim to be 'The Fifty Shilling Tailors'. It is probable that Rational Tailoring supported Leicester's first, and for 200 years only industry, by selling men's socks and other hosiery. For years the hosiery industry had employed the majority of workers in Leicester. By the advent of the first world war, handframe knitters had all but disappeared and were being replaced by knitting machines. Despite this, hosiery jobs in the East Midlands rose from 50,000 in 1911 to 77,000 in 1939 and Leicester, because of its prosperity in this area, became known as the 'Boom City'.

Bottom: Does this view of the White Hart Hotel take you back? Many readers will remember the distinctive black and white facade of the White Hart Inn. The building used to be a familiar sight to the people of Leicester and one which, because of its longevity, was inevitably and naturally taken for granted. However, this photograph of the Hotel was taken from the Clock Tower in 1958 and has preserved forever this nostalgic piece of Leicester's history. The term 'public house' was not utilised until the early years of the 17th century. Only then did the phrase come into common usage when referring to all inns, taverns and alehouses. Later, during the Victorian era, the term was shortened to 'pub' and was used to describe the descendants of the inn. Before becoming a hotel however, the White Hart was always known as an inn and had been a constant fixture in the Haymarket for centuries. For a period during the 1700s the Inn temporarily branched out into the complimentary business of coaching which, although novel at the time, was a certain money-maker. By 1787, the White Hart Inn was operating at least six journeys a week to London. The advent of the railways kept the inn in business and trade flourishing as passengers and railwaymen alike needed a place to rest and relax. Sadly however, after becoming a hotel, the White Hart was eventually demolished as part of a redevelopment scheme to make way for a Littlewoods store.

Earning a crust

In 1903 Leicester Corporation made the decision to spend an estimated £650,000 converting from horse tramcars to electric ones. The colossal undertaking of preparing the streets of the town for this conversion began and roads were closed whilst their surfaces were dug up and tracks were laid. The extent of the consequent disruption can be glimpsed in this photograph of the laying of the tramlines at the Clock Tower. Here, the size of the task was magnified because of the amount of traffic that usually circled the Tower. Remarkably however, the work, including the lifting of old horse tramway rails and the addition of hardwood blocks, was completed in just ten days The opening ceremony was held on 18th May 1904 and signalled the beginning of a new electric era. A fleet of double-deck, open-top tramcars in a deep maroon livery operated a public service from the Clock Tower to the depot. The new tramways proved to be a resounding success with the people of Leicester and over the following years more and more trams were added to the fleet and many improvements made. However, both world wars took their toll on the system and with the advent of motor buses, the trams became redundant. In 1949 the last tramcar completed its run and was appropriately decorated with the words, 'We mourn the loss of faithful friends, from the streets of our grand old city. To move with the times, we cannot have lines, so - go they must - it's a pity'!

This British Council photograph shows no ordinary hospital ward. Unusually, these hospital beds have been wheeled out onto a covered terrace allowing the patients to convalesce in the fresh air and sunshine. One of Leicester's oldest hospitals, no longer to be seen, was Wyggeston's Hospital founded by William Wyggeston in 1513. William Wyggeston was a member of Leicester's richest family at the beginning of the 16th century and had made his fortune in the wool trade. William was, in fact, Leicester's richest man and in 1524, he paid 22 per cent of the town's tax! William was Mayor of Leicester twice as well as being an MP several times and four times the Mayor of Calais. An influential and powerful man, William was also, to a certain extent, a philanthropist. In 1511 he and his brothers founded the chantry house in the Newarke and just two years later William himself founded Wyggeston's Hospital. The hospital provided care for 12 poor men and 12 poor women who were required to pray for the soul of their benefactor. The patients admitted could not just have any illness they had to be, 'blind, lame, decrepit, paralytic or maimed of their limbs, or idiots wanting their natural senses, so that they be peaceable, not disturbing the hospital'! The hospital was demolished in 1875 and Leicester Grammar School now stands on the site. A new hospital was erected on Fosse Road South and the buildings on that site are still supported by the Wyggeston Foundation.

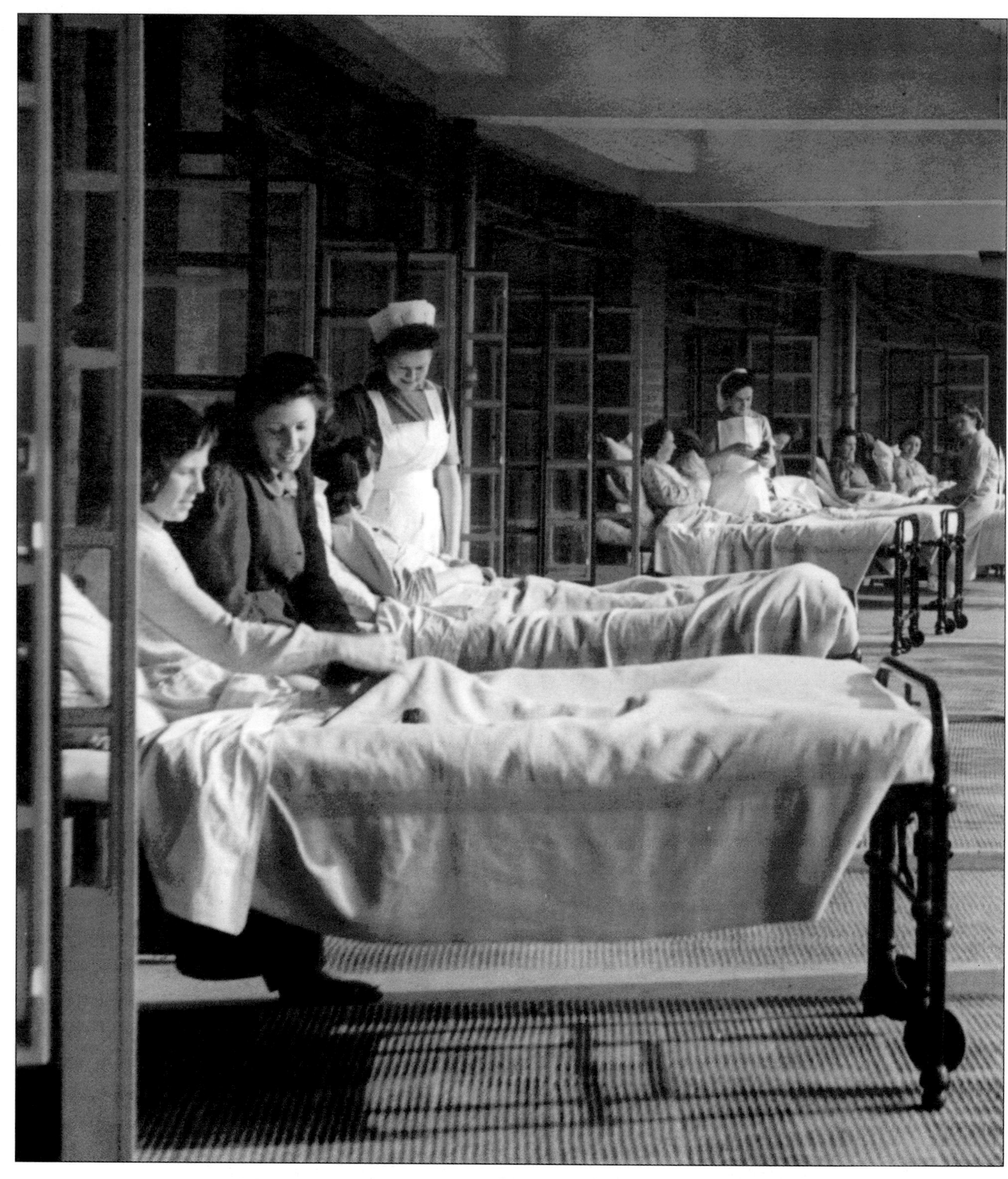

Following the track to the top

'Caterpillar' track-type tractors first came to the attention of the Great British public in the rather unfortunate context of the first world war, when tremendous optimism surrounded the Allies' new weapon, the tank. Shipped to France in crates marked 'water tanks' - a clever ploy to confuse the enemy - these armoured vehicles were first used on 15th December at the Battle of the Somme, and their caterpillar tracks enabled them to travel over terrain that wheeled vehicles could never have crossed. This part of the story is often told, but fewer people know that the track-type tractors had been developed by Benjamin Holt, an American who during the 1890s had experimented with various forms of steam tractors for use in farming. At around the same time another American, Daniel Best, was conducting similar experiments, and in 1925 the two men merged their respective companies to form the Caterpillar Tractor Company.

By the mid-20th century Caterpillar's assembly line in East Peoria, from which the Diesel Sixty Tractor had first rolled in 1931, was producing a variety of graders and other equipment, and the company was ready to expand its markets by moving into the United Kingdom. It built a parts factory in Coalville in 1950/51, but just three years later this site had been outgrown and the Caterpillar Tractor Company Limited relocated to Desford, where it took over the former Aerodrome. Here the workforce continued to grow, and in 1969 the factory began to manufacture complete fork lift trucks as well as replacement parts.

A spell of intense competition in the lift truck market resulted in Caterpillar (UK) Ltd, as the company was now known, commenced manufacturing Backhoe Loaders (diggers) in 1983. This signified a change of direction for the Leicester plant; it was recognised that the future lay in smaller, easier-to-handle vehicles, and this is still reflected in Leicester's current product list. Backhoe loaders, small wheel loaders, telehandlers, compact wheel loaders and mini hydraulic excavators are produced in Desford and exported all over the world.

The year 2000 marked Caterpillar's 50th successful year in the UK. Caterpillar (UK) Ltd has become far more than a production area; it is a full development facility, with state-of-the-art computer design facilities, full product prototyping and engineering capabilities, and access to some of the most advanced research and development facilities in the world. With two Queen's Awards for Export Achievement and the prestigious Investors in People Award to its name, the company is committed to keeping the emphasis on quality, and maintaining, through its valued workforce, Caterpillar's position as one of the most recognised names in the world.

Top right: *Demonstrating a fork lift truck in the late 1960s.* ***Left:*** *Fork lift maintenance in progress.* ***Below:*** *The firm's Leicester premises.*

Building - a family business

The story of Jelson Limited, and its rise to prominence as an award-winning house-builder, regarded today as one of the leading employers of the East Midlands, is a tale of family endeavour, self-reliance, a commitment to crafts-manship and, perhaps most of all, to an abiding bond of loyalty between management and workforce. 'Once a Jelson man, always a Jelson man' went the phrase, and even today, when long service with a single employer has become all but a thing of the past, nearly 100 staff can boast over 25 years uninterrupted experience with the firm. The roots to this remarkable state of affairs go back a long, long way.

In 1889, James Jelley, the 24 year old son of an engineer was living with his wife at 43 Shenton Street, Leicester and decided to set up in business on his own account as a self-employed joiner and shopfitter. Operating from his home, the business soon prospered and by 1897 employed seven staff. Extensive travel was a strong feature of these early days, as James began to generate work - principally in shopfitting - throughout the region. His diligence paid off, and as joinery and shopfitting contracts started to flow in, the business was able to offer a growing range of services. By the early 1900s, James Jelley was also making a name for himself as an undertaker. In the years that followed, Shenton Street was enlarged to cope with increased amounts of activity - stables at the rear of adjoining houses were developed to house a machine shop on the ground floor and a joinery workshop above, while the firm was also able to acquire stores on the other side of Shenton Street, in addition to a funeral parlour and shop in nearby Charnwood Street.

A more fundamental growth in the company's fortunes accompanied the arrival at the firm of James' son. Herbert Jelley served with the Leicestershire Yeomanry during the First World War, in White Russia for a time, and had also received a grounding as an apprentice with a Leicester firm of builders and joiners.

Discharged from the army in 1919, he shortly afterwards began to work with his father and almost immediately showed a keen aptitude for the building business. With his sister, Florence (later Mrs Stubbings), at his side - taking responsibility for office work and sales - Herbert soon had a building operation up and running. Early projects consisted of single houses, or pairs, in the Humberstone area of Leicester - and under Herbert's able stewardship,

***Above:** Herbert Jelley, son of the founder, James Jelley, who joined the family business in 1919.* ***Below:** One of Jelson's developments in the 1940s serviced by the firm's own fleet of machinery and transport.*

the new venture was soon flourishing, while his father continued to concentrate his efforts on the joinery, shopfitting and undertaking side of the business. By 1925, J Jelley & Son were already firmly established as a sought-after local builder employing around 40 staff in the joinery shops and on a growing number of building sites.

Herbert lived in Greenland Drive in Leicester and is remembered as a forthright yet fair individual, much respected in the local community. He was apparently a 'stickler for good time-keeping' but inspired unfailing loyalty amongst the workforce by many acts of kindness and a genuine concern for their welfare. Every Friday afternoon, he would visit all the sites with a Gladstone bag and personally hand out wages to each of the men, and when one employee, Walter Wincott, was keen to buy his first company-built house in 1934, Herbert even arranged to guarantee his mortgage. While the depression hit many firms in the 1930s, J Jelley & Son continued to prosper - through a combination of benevolent management and an unrivalled reputation for dependable, high-quality workmanship.

If Herbert was a model employer, he was also a businessman of considerable acumen and enterprise. By the late 1920s, the local authority was increasingly turning to J Jelley & Son for the construction of Leicester Corporation housing estates; but Herbert was looking ahead and becoming interested in the scope for private housing development. With characteristic foresight, he began a process of land acquisition, seizing opportunities to purchase parcels, a few acres at a time, for future building schemes on the outskirts of Leicester. A ready market for private housing was further enhanced by forging productive links with local building societies, and within a few short years J Jelley's own housing construction became the firm's main activity. Before the outbreak of war in 1939, annual output had risen to 400-500 properties on a number of sites, the largest being at Wyngate Drive/Hinckley Road. The average price at that time for a typical semi-detached house was in the region of £375 - while a weekly wage for an apprentice was around 10/2d (51p) for a 48 hour week.

Top: *The original premises at 43 Shenton Street, Leicester.* ***Left:*** *Florence Stubbings who, along with her brother, helped build a successful business.*

New home-owners in the mid-1930s were demonstrating a modern appetite for self-reliance and a relish for independence and autonomy in their lives. J Jelley & Son, meanwhile, were beginning to manifest a similar philosophy in their approach to business. As their house-building activities grew, so the joinery division in Shenton Street expanded until it was eventually able to supply all the major timber components used in Jelley houses. Herbert's purchase, in 1932, of the firm's first mechanical excavator also marked the start of a process that would lead eventually to the current modern fleet of internal plant, enabling the company to tackle virtually any on-site task without recourse to subcontractors.

By 1939, the business had set its course for the future. By now, it was predominantly a house-builder, with other departments given over almost entirely to supporting that role. Although some shopfitting was still undertaken, the funeral parlour had to be disposed of. There was an atmosphere of exciting change and new beginnings - but it was also the end of an era, made all the more poignant by the death in 1938 of James Jelley. He worked assiduously right up to the end, at the heart of an enterprise he had himself founded - very nearly fifty years before. If there was any immediate comfort for his loved ones it was that at least the company itself would survive, under the able command of his son, Herbert.

War broke out - and everything changed. Mortgage funds dried up as building societies ceased lending and J Jelley & Son found themselves at work on houses for which there could be no buyers. There was only one solution and that was to let them, as they were finished, in order to recoup at least some of the building costs

Above: *Some of the employees who were the driving force in the joinery works.* ***Below:*** *An advertisement for the original range of shop fronts and shop fittings that the firm made.*

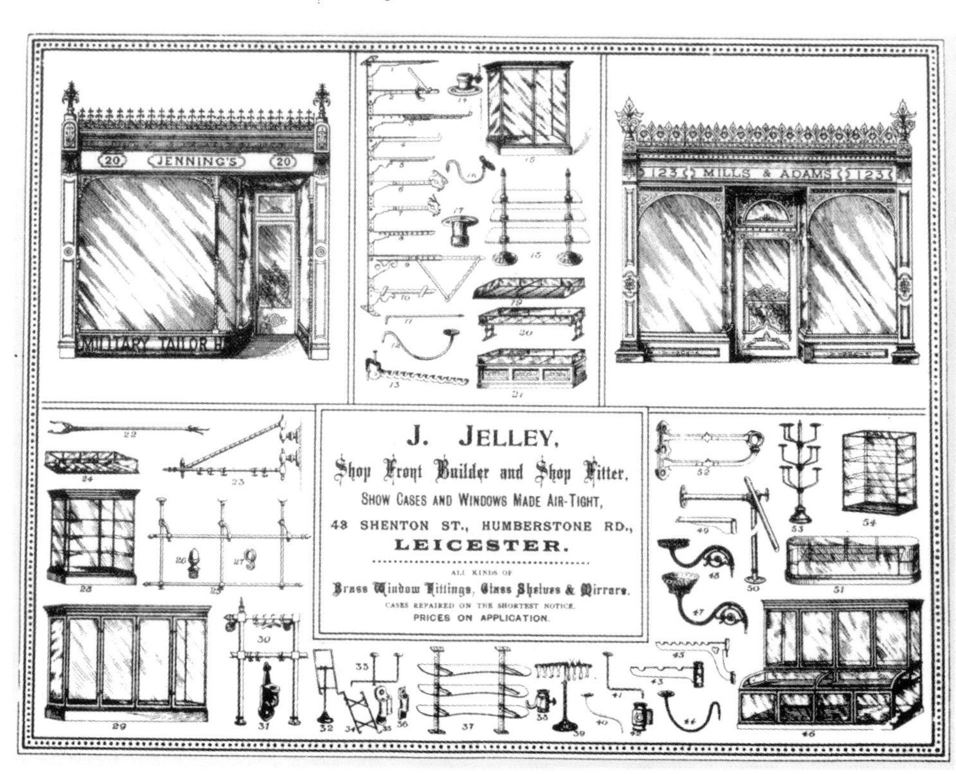

until they could be sold. It's an interesting fact, however, that some of those lettings survive to this day - an odd little feature in the company but a tangible reminder of wartime vicissitudes.

Private housing development ground inevitably to a halt, and many Jelley staff were called up for military service - but it turned out to be a busy few years for the company. Factories in the Midlands were turned over to essential war work and J Jelley & Son were soon actively involved in maintenance and reconstruction tasks on industrial sites throughout the region. Bombing raids wrought devastation in a number of towns, and J Jelley & Son were able to supply gangs of skilled workers throughout the war to assist with rebuilding. At one point, the firm had 80 men travelling by lorry from Leicester to Coventry each day, and 40 to Nuneaton. Unusual jobs during this period included the construction of stands for the visit of King George VI and Queen Elizabeth to inspect the war damage - and the building of the first two British Restaurants in Coventry, where people could enjoy a meal for about one shilling (5p).

In Leicester, meanwhile, the firm - using its own agricultural equipment - converted some of its sites at Narborough Road, Wigston and at Scapcroft for crop production!

Business remained brisk, and varied. But there was tragedy too when Herbert's elder son, Leonard - already a member of the firm - was killed in Burma in 1944. It therefore fell to his younger brother, Ronald, to continue the family tradition and he joined the company as an apprentice joiner as the war came to an end. Herbert's immediate objective, at the end of hostilities, was to resume normal business activity as quickly as possible. Florence, still active at her desk, wrote innumerable letters to all former staff who had been on military service with a single request: 'when can you start back?'. And men returned in their droves at the first opportunity, to set about a host of projects which mushroomed as peace returned. Repairing war damage was a vital task in Leicester as in so many other towns after the war, and although the government imposed an embargo on private housing development, there was huge investment targeted on Local Authority housing schemes. J Jelley & Son won several large contracts to build houses both in the city and in the county as a whole. One of the first major jobs was the construction of a hundred houses at Woodhouse Eaves to provide homes for workers - some from Cyprus - who had been recruited to the War Department Signals Depot at Garrats Hay.

By 1947, with a loyal and industrious workforce in place, a turning point was reached for the business when a private limited company was formed to take over the assets of the family firm. This significant step was accompanied by a change of name - and from this time onwards, the business has been known as Jelson Limited. A new era was over the horizon, and the next decade was to see the company making dynamic strides forward under its chairman, Herbert Jelley. Whilst the embargo on private housing construction persisted, the company tendered successfully for other projects, including work on schools, factories and offices. This experience was to provide a useful background to diversification in the modern era, but in the early 1950s - when private housing schemes were again permitted, Jelson fell to the task with renewed

Below: *Newly invested club members at the Quarter Century Club Dinner in 1988, with the Chairman seated in the centre.*

enthusiasm. Expansion across the East Midlands saw a growing workforce required on a number of different sites, and the company was swift to purchase buses to move labour to Uppingham - and later to purchase vans based in Uppingham for use in Peterborough and Stamford. At one time, it was said that Jelson had 'more buses than the Corporation!'

It was soon apparent that the Shenton Street premises were inadequate to support the new levels of business activity. In 1957, work began on its present headquarters at 370 Loughborough Road, accommodating on its three acre site a modern office block, a purpose built joinery unit and a depot for a growing fleet of plant and vehicles.

By the 1960s, Jelson Limited had become a building force to be reckoned with. Operating from its Leicester base across some 26 sites spread into Rutland and Lincolnshire, the next 20 years saw the number of completed houses reach 10,000 units in the 1960s and 9,000 in the 1970s. Smaller house and bungalow developments were now only part of the story, as Jelson embarked on a number of architect designed properties in higher price ranges. Commercial and public customers also increased in number with a variety of major building and civil engineering projects coming Jelson's way. Self-reliance remained a company characteristic - as it does today - and was typified at this time by the supply of sand and gravel from Jelson's own pits - four of which were brought into operation in Leicestershire in the early 1960s. While other builders were slimming down their direct labour forces, Jelson's own saw a period of expansion and the workforce grew to 750.

Above: *A view of the Jelson Group premises at 370 Loughborough Road, Leicester.* ***Below:*** *An example of the latest type of architect designed property built by Jelson at Swithland.*

When Herbert Jelley died, after a period of illness, in 1963, the reins were taken up by his son, Ronald who successfully steered the business to still greater success. The completion of the Leicestershire village of East Goscote was a notable achievement. Conceived as an entire community, and unique in its day, it was based on a 140 acre site, between Queniborough and Rearsby. Formerly the home of a government munitions factory, and subsequently a store, Jelson acquired the land by auction and then set about the elaborate job of demolishing all the old buildings and developing and landscaping the site to provide a full range of village amenities - including a school, shops, pub, village hall and industrial units.

In more recent years, innovative projects have embraced the refurbishment and conversion of older properties for the modern lifestyle. A particularly interesting example has been the Parklands development in Sleaford, on the site of an ancient Roman burial ground and mint, which included the refurbishment of an historical manor house - the 'Old Place' - reputedly haunted by the ghost of Lord Hussey who was executed in 1538. Nothing untoward is believed to have occurred in the course of this work! - and the result is a remarkable celebration of our historic past achieved by means of the most modern building techniques.

Jelson Ltd celebrates its own proud traditions too and continues to place the greatest emphasis on the importance of people. The family atmosphere, for which the firm is renowned, remains as inspirational today as it has always been - and great store is still laid by long service. The company's Quarter Century Club which has, amongst its 180 members, both retired and current staff boasting over 25 years employment with the firm, has become a popular forum for reminiscence and renewed friendships. Each November the club holds a dinner in Leicester and sees new members welcomed, each one presented with an inscribed gold watch.

Jelson Limited has long been recognised as one of the leading House Builders in the East Midlands and over recent years has received many awards for its work. As we commence a new millennium the Company received the top honour at the prestigious House Builder of the Year Awards organised by Express Newspapers. The Company scooped the Gold Trophy for the second year running in the category of housebuilders building 251 - 750 homes each year. Entrants in the competition were judged by their own customers which clearly demonstrates that the traditional building methods, standards of craftsmanship and family values associated with Jelson Limited are as important today as they have been over the last hundred years.

Top: *House Builder of the Year Awards won by Jelson between 1998 and 2000.*
Below: *A typical Jelson street scene.*

History in the making - The Shires, Leicester's super shopping centre

History does not relate only to events which happened a very long time ago. Our world changes a little each day until the slow but steady accumulation of those changes makes us suddenly realise that the local environment has changed dramatically within our own lifetimes. In truth history begins with yesterday.

Since it first opened its doors to the public in August 1991 the Shires Shopping Centre has become known as one of the East Midlands' leading retail fashion shopping centres.

Right: *This shows the centre under construction, the nearest point being St Peters Lane with Bond Street to the left and High Street Junction at the top of the picture. The Lewis Tower is also clearly visible, which was retained when the rest of the former Department Store was demolished to make way for the Haymarket Towers development.*
Below: *The main entrance showing the retained Victorian facade at Eastgates.*

The site now occupied by the Shires Centre formed the original heart of Leicester dating back to Roman times. Highcross Street at the west end of the Shires at its junction with High Street was the central point of Leicester. To this day many of the original gates to the historic city are still identified, the nearest to the centre being Churchgate which forms the eastern boundary of the Shires site.

In 1989 pre-construction work on the £125 million Shires project provided an opportunity for two archaeological digs within the site boundaries. During the course of those excavations items unearthed included the remains of Roman roads and a variety of medieval and Tudor artefacts. Further Roman remains were unearthed in the area of Churchgate when the second phase of the centre was built in 1992.

High Street had for many years already been the principal shopping street of Leicester and included the very large Co-op department store which had itself occupied a significant part of the Shires' site for many decades. Extensive propping was called for during demolition work to retain the Victorian facade of the old Co-op. That wonderful facade now forms the High Street frontage of the centre's second major anchor store - House of Fraser-Rackhams.

Foundation work for the new shopping centre included approximately 1,200 concrete piles sunk to an average depth of 12m. The superstructure of the Shires is a mix of in-situ and pre-cast concrete, steelwork and reinforced concrete floor beams. Ibstock bricks and re-constituted stone were used for much of the external finishes.

In 1992 the second phase was made possible by the purchase of several small properties on Churchgate through to Bond Street. Deep excavations there revealed a marble staircase and rooms from an old department store which had been bricked up for years. That second phase gave access to the Shires' lower trading floor and created a new link to the main mall.

The shopping mall is on two levels with a central concourse linked to the High Street by climate- controlled glazed malls. The central concourse, which is over a hundred metres long, features a solar reflecting roof some

Top: *The Central Main Concourse - West End Centre.* ***Above left:*** *Current day aerial view of The Shires Shopping Centre. The main concourse is clearly visible with its green tinted glass roof. Covering a site in total of some nine acres, the centre can clearly be seen to occupy a prime position in the very heart of the city centre. The clock tower can be seen central right of the picture.*

21 metres high; this space provides access to the shops on the 'trading floors' and is intersected by two glazed bridges linking the car park levels to the shops.

One of the bridges features eight cascading escalators connecting all five levels and the other a scenic lift, there are also two passenger lifts at the west end of the centre giving easy customer access between the centre's three deck multi-storey car park and the two shopping malls below. Another interesting feature, a reminder of just how times have moved on in this hi-tech age, is that the Centre's lighting is designed for automatic adjustment to reflect the time of day and season.

In addition to more than 80 shop units of varying sizes the Shires also features two department stores. One, covering 16,400 square metres, is occupied by Debenhams and the second, covering 14,000 square metres, by House of Fraser-Rackhams.

Due to the large scale of the development it was necessary to have a number of special features incorporated into the building to ensure the safety of the public

Above: *Les Dennis pictured when he lit the Christmas lights in the late 1990s.* ***Top:*** *A main entrance to the centre on High Street.*

in additional to the usual fire escapes and fire exits. Those measures include a full smoke control system in the malls - achieved by both natural and mechanical ventilation; the installation of automatic fire shutters to the major department stores at the junction with the mall; a complete sprinkler system to all parts of the building used for retail purposes including the malls, and lastly a full alarm system has been installed throughout the building.

In the years since its opening the Shires has contributed greatly to the now widespread perception of Leicester city centre as a major regional shopping destination and has succeeded in creating a new direction for Leicester. The history of the Shires Centre can be traced back to the mid nineteen eighties when the Leicester Co—operative society first made an approach to a company called CLE Southern (a firm later bought out by the Imry Group) to discuss the feasibility of building a shopping centre to incorporate the then Co-op in the High street. The scheme eventually delivered, ironically no longer featuring the Co-op, however took some years to reach fruition. The gestation period included long discussions with the City Council, a body naturally concerned that such a large development should not have a deleterious impact on the city centre.

Not surprisingly the developers felt that the High Street was the natural location for a new shopping centre - historically it was the main retailing street in the city. And no insurmountable construction problems with the site had been found. After due discussion and debate wholehearted support was eventually received from the City Council, support which ultimately helped ensure the success of the project.

The whole of site, parts of which were previously an open car park , the Co-op's department store and a miscellaneous collection of other buildings, were all eventually purchased by the developers in partnership with Leicester City Council. All the buildings, with the exception of the Co-op facade, and the building on it's Eastgate frontage were subsequently demolished.

Left: *Lisa Riley and Sammy Shire, the centre's mascot, switching on the Christmas lights in 1999.* ***Below:*** *A Wedding Fayre which took place in 1999.*

Plans for the new construction were prepared by Chapman Taylor partners, one of the most experienced shopping centre design firms in the country.

Once building permission had been granted building the new centre proceeded rapidly. In May 1991 Debenhams opened and this was followed by the phased opening of both malls over the next few months. Rackhams opened in February 1992 with the Centre being fully let by November 1993. A final extension to the Shires was completed in December 1994 providing another primary entrance to the Centre containing a Virgin Megastore and Waterstones Booksellers.

The whole shopping centre provides an astonishing 550,000 square feet of retail space within the 9.5 acre site. And it has certainly proved popular - within two years of opening almost fifteen million customers a year were visiting the centre increasing by another million during the following year. The car park too also proved it was needed with three quarters of million cars being parked there annually by 1993.

Perhaps most welcome of all to shoppers in this age of the motor car was the provision of that new city centre car park. The Shires' 920 space car park gained a gold award from the police and AA in November 1992 for the security features it incorporated. The car park was visited in early 2000 by Minister and Home Secretary Jack Straw - and led the way to a national campaign for greater security in car parks throughout the whole country.

In addition to security another important feature is the provision of access for disabled people. The Shires Shopping Centre was designed from the outset to allow the disabled access to all parts of the building including lifts between floors. As required by the building regulations, where stair's are also provided within the shops these are designed for use by ambulant disabled people as are all the toilet facilities provided for use by the public and for staff employed within the centre. In March 1994 'Shopmobility' relocated to the Shires to provide better facilities for the disabled of Leicester. Shopmobility is situated on level 2 near Debenhams: motorised and manual wheel chairs are available for those who would like to make use of them. The Shopmobilty scheme is operated by Leicester City Council and volunteer helpers.

Outside the public areas and rarely noted by the passing shoppers, there are also four remote service yards situated at all points of the compass round the centre which give direct access by service lifts and corridors to all of the centre's retail areas.

Considerable thought was given to finding ways with which to establish the initial and continuing high standards within the Shires Centre. Leases are broken down into various sections depending on square footage. On the tenants' side there are restrictions on how and what they can trade, the design and quality of their shops, the stocks they may hold and sell. Both parties have to comply with the company's rules - for example the tenants have to trade during the opening hours of the centre, they are not permitted to exhibit posters, play loud music and must keep their premises clean and tidy. In return the landlord covenants to guarantee them the quiet enjoyment of good services, i.e. security, cleaning, maintenance of the building generally and agrees not to interfere unnecessarily with the tenants and their right to trade.

Security, cleaning and general maintenance are handled in- house; waste disposal is contracted to T Watts a local waste disposal company.

The Centre has a strong advertising and promotions section. It advertises in all media outlets, newspapers, radio and television at different times of the year depending upon the campaign, for example, Spring, Summer, Autumn and Christmas. The television airtime covers Central, West and East regions. There are also fashion shows held on a regular basis designed to entice ever more customers to visit the Shires.

The Centre also retains a public relations company which deals directly with the media and works with the Centre Management in sending out press releases

Above: *The Ice clock tower which featured in a competition to guess how many coins were on the clock face and also how long the structure would melt.*

for various events and matters connected with the centre. Locally Shires Management is a actively involved with various organisations and local authorities , the City Council, statutory authorities, schools, colleges, the British Red Cross, a charity of the year, disabled groups and many other voluntary groups; the Shires management aims to ensure that the centre is a fundamental part of the local community.

Running costs of the Shires Shopping Centre are in excess of a million pounds each year. But, no doubt surprisingly to many, Shires Management, the company established to look after the centre on a day to day basis is a non-profit making entity.

The wider management structure originally comprised the London based developers Imry Holdings Ltd which owned both the Shires Centre and subsequently Shires Management Ltd as a wholly owned subsidiary.

In March 1997 however ownership changed, the new joint owners being Rodamco United Kingdom BV and Possfund Custodian Ltd, with asset management being undertaken by DTZ Debenham Tie Leung (London).

The current Shires management team, based on the Shires site, comprises Doug Owles the Centre Manager also in charge of marketing; a veteran with over twenty years of shopping centre experience he spent 13 year in Milton Keynes before coming to Leicester during the development stage of the Shires Centre. David Exley is Operations Manager and Sam Dowdall is PA and Marketing Assistant.

Nothing stands still at the Shires: in the late nineteen nineties Sunday trading was introduced in response to a shift in the public's shopping patterns. No longer just a chore, shopping has become a family day out with mum, dad and the children often meeting at the Shires for a complete day spent at the centre.

The management team has responded to those new challenges by actively striving to make the Shires more attractive than ever, for example launching a children's loyalty club, staging competitions and other attractions such as celebrity guests. Over the years such famous visitors have included Dale Winton, Lisa Riley, Brian Blessed, Les Dennis and everyone's favourite Disney Characters Mickey and Minnie Mouse to name but a few.

Perhaps those who have used the Shires will recall the Ice clock tower competition and of having tried to guess how many coins were on the clock face. On this occasion those who correctly guessed how many coins were featured stood to win a prize of £100 whilst those who correctly forecast how long it would take for the ice structure to melt stood to gain £1,000!

What the future holds for Leicester we cannot say, but as far as the Shires Shopping Centre is concerned we have, this time at least, been privileged to witness the City's history in the making.

Left: *Doug Owles, centre manager, celebrating the second year of Sunday Trading in 1998.*
Below: *Leicester's Mayor and local artist Olwen Hughes launch the Millennium Banners scheme with local schoolchildren.*

Building Leicester

The history of all towns and cities is one of continuous change. The appearance of Leicester has changed enormously over the last two centuries and one of the principal agents of that change has been the Leicester firm of consulting engineers and architects, Pick Everard.

Founded by one man in 1866 today Pick Everard is a leading multi-professional practice embracing the specialised skills of water engineering, public health and environmental engineering, architecture, planning, mechanical and electrical engineering, structural engineering and surveying.

Over its many decades of continuous practice the firm has been responsible for a huge number of building and engineering projects. The firm's advice and design services have been called upon by government departments, public authorities, business and industry alike across all parts of the United Kingdom. Pick Everard offers a versatile consultancy service of the highest standard, provided by friendly, well-qualified and experienced staff. This forms an 'umbrella service' looking at every aspect of professional advice that clients may require within the broad area of building and engineering construction.

The majority of the firm's work has been in the United Kingdom but as opportunities have arisen the business has undertaken projects in the USA, Nigeria, China, South Africa, Europe and the Irish Republic.

The firm was founded in Leicester in 1866 by John Breedon Everard - an ambitious young man and one who was eventually to become High Sheriff of Leicestershire. Over the following decade JB Everard steadily established himself as both an architect and engineer.

John Breedon Everard had been an assistant resident engineer building the St Pancras railway station for the Midland Railway Company. In a few short years he had learned a great deal about mining and engineering. Armed with his civil engineering skills he returned to his Leicestershire roots, got married and moved into a fashionable area of Leicester, De Montfort Street.

JB Everard had taken a number of private commissions whilst working for the Midland Railway Company and although until 1868 he had to return to London three times each week he was, on the strength of his earlier private work, soon able to build up his own practice in Leicester.

At that time John Breedon's skills were almost unique in the Midlands. At the age of only 27 he won his first major contract - the new Leicester Cattle Market, built to replace the old one in the town centre. The new cattle market was opened in 1872. The Cattle Market Committee determined the rates for its new charges, which ranged from one shilling for a stallion down to one penny for a suckling pig - and were based in the market's counting house, where the pennies and shillings were collected, and which is now a public house.

John Breedon Everard prospered, not least as a result of a range of important legislation in the late nineteenth century, particularly the Public Health Act of 1875 concerned with health, water, housing and town planning. By 1888 the firm had grown to eight employees. In 1892 JB Everard had been appointed as consulting engineer for Leicester's water supply - an appointment which quickly led to new opportunities for water supply, drainage

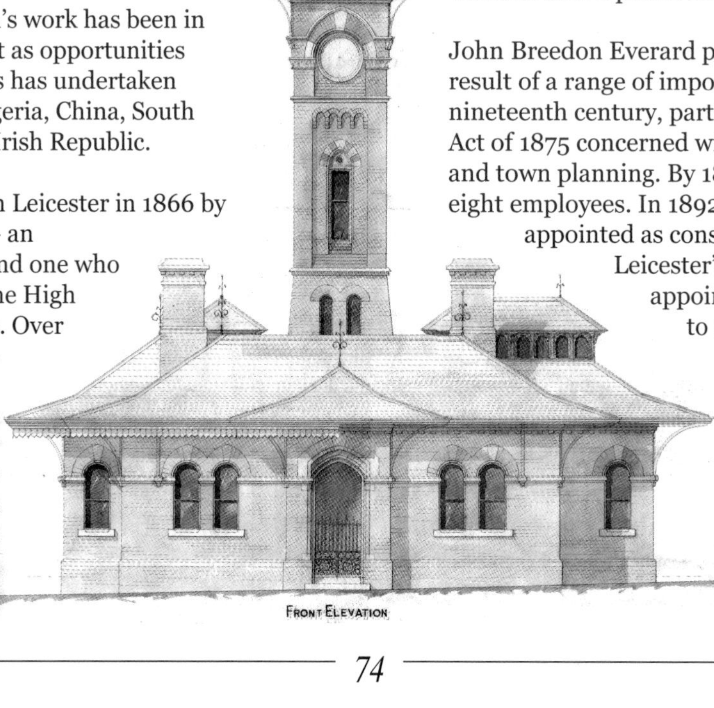

***Top left:** S Perkins Pick and J B Everard. **Top right:** Martin Gimson. **Above:** William Keay. **Left:** The Counting House, Leicester Cattle Market, 1872.*

Kibworth, Samuel P Pick joined Everard as an assistant in 1882 and was taken into partnership six years later, a role he was to occupy until 1919.

Samuel Pick soon made his presence felt in the partnership, designing the Thomas Pares Bank in St Martin's, now a listed building. Until recently the building was still being used by the NatWest Bank; Skillington's History of Leicester (1923) described the building as 'amongst the most dignified and inspiring monuments in Leicester'.

Samuel Pick also built the practice's excellent reputation in the field of health care, gained during the first world war designing recovery wards for disabled and wounded soldiers. He worked on the designs for various lunatic asylums and hospitals including major development work at the Leicester Royal Infirmary where Pick Everard continue to work to this day.

and sewage disposal schemes beyond the boundaries of Leicestershire. From 1898 - 99 John Everard worked tirelessly to negotiate the Leicester Water Bill and designed a major aquaduct scheme to allow water to be transferred from the River Derwent in Derbyshire to support the needs of the growing city.

The 'Pick' half of the firm's name is a reminder of Samuel Perkins Pick. Born in Kettering but schooled in

John Everard remained with the firm until retirement in 1911 and lived on until 1923, having watched from the sidelines as his firm survived the difficult years of the first world war - not the least of which was the reduction in staff numbers due to military service.

Top: *Aylestone mains drainage, 1946.*
Left: *Thomas Pares Bank, 1898.*
Below: *The Imperial Typewriters building, 1923.*

From the latter part of the nineteenth century, the firm acted as County Architects and Engineers to Leicester Corporation and continued to do so for over fifty years until the council formed its own architects' and engineers' departments in 1948.

Amongst the firm's best known local works during its early years are the Swithland Reservoir (1894) and Carlton Hayes Hospital (1899) - then the Leicester and Rutland Lunatic Asylum and now the site of the Headquarters of the Alliance and Leicester.

The Swithland reservoir project was to be the first and only dam built by JB Everard. It was, however, a major undertaking, employing 500 men to construct the 500 million gallon capacity reservoir. In more recent times Pick Everard has worked in co-operation with other firms to create Rutland Water.

William Keay became a partner in 1911 having begun work for the firm in 1888. Keay eventually was to become Director of Architecture at the Leicester College of Art and Technology and later gave a 20 year endowment for the best student at the college.

Keay, a water specialist, became senior partner in 1919 following the death of Samuel Pick and was to dominate the partnership for 33 years until his own retirement in 1948, having been County Architect and Engineer until that time. William Keay's son Cyril joined the partnership in 1923. One of Cyril's most important achievements was to be the Imperial Typewriter factory in East Park Road, Leicester.

Right: *DeMontfort University, Hawthorn Building 1896.* ***Below:*** *Sawley Aqueduct, 1907.*

Martin Gimson joined the firm in the same year as Cyril Keay. It was Martin Gimson who built up the firm's particular expertise in water and sewerage work during the inter war years and lead to their involvement in such major projects as flood prevention work in the River Sence, viaducts in the Derwent valley and the Ladybower Reservoir. It was around this time that the firm became known as Pick Everard Keay and Gimson

The face of Leicester and Leicestershire was being constantly changed by the work of the firm. Following the second world war in addition to being involved in housing projects throughout Rutland, Leicestershire and Northamptonshire the firm designed the award winning Leicester University's Astley Clarke Building, the Leicester Temperance Building Society at Halford House in Charles Street - now the firms headquarters, Norwich Union House in Horsefair Street, the East Midland Gas Board offices and showrooms, The Leicester Mercury printing works and offices, the Royal Insurance building in Charles Street and the redevelopment of Leicester Royal Infirmary as a teaching hospital.

From the mid-1970s as the organisation of clients in many government and local authority departments changed, Pick Everard expanded into regional offices in Bury St Edmunds and Taunton. In recent years further offices have been added in Glasgow, Bath and Inverness to provide a truly nationwide service. Communication with clients has also changed beyond recognition. Design drawings that once used to be produced on parchment and waxed linen as traditional blueprints are now produced by designers with the aid of computer technology, and can be transmitted to clients worldwide at the press of a button.

Pick Everard continue to change and enhance the landscape of the city. Recent examples of the work of the practice within Leicester can be seen at Hamilton New Town, Oadby Racecourse, Grove Park, DeMontfort University, and Leicester Royal Infirmary. As part of their 125th anniversary celebrations in 1991, the firm funded the refurbishment of the Clock Tower.

All these are visible reminders of the work of the practice. However, just as bringing a clean water supply and sanitation was one of the first major achievements of John Breedon Everard so, underground and hidden away, are the many water pipes, sewers and treatment plants designed by Pick Everard to ensure the continuing welfare of the people of Leicester.

Today the firm's main markets in the UK are still public health projects, educational facilities, health care, retail and commercial projects, leisure, and military accommodation as well as roads and infrastructure. Overseas markets include hotels, primary infrastructure and industrial manufacturing. The firm's main clients include water companies, major retailers, insurance companies, universities, local authorities, government departments and developers.

Pick Everard which employed just eight people at the end of the first world war has seen continuous growth over the course of its very long history and now employs over 200 staff.

The firm's unique selling points today, as in the past, are its broad multi-professional capability for design and project management over a wide variety of building types and forms of construction. Pick Everard's business philosophy is to be at the leading edge of multi-discipline design consultancy with the ability to adapt and respond quickly to the changing needs of clients.

***Above:** Tattersalls Grandstand, Leicester Racecourse, 1997. **Left:** Oadby Superstore, 1998. **Below:** Senior partners taking the firm forward into the 21st century.*

From pubs to palaces

What do pubs, ships and palaces all have in common? At one time or another craftsmen from the Leicester firm of E E Smith Contracts Ltd have had a hand in creating or maintaining interiors for all of them.

Within the UK EE Smith Contracts Ltd is one of only a handful of large specialist fitting out companies capable of carrying out complete interior contracts costing as much as five million pounds.

The company was founded by Edward Elija Smith in around 1897. At first Edward Smith ran his business from a small shop in Canning Street. A typical moustachioed Victorian craftsman the original EE Smith described himself on his letterheads as not only a 'plumber, gas and bar fitter' but also a master craftsman and advertised that he supplied and repaired gas stoves and gas chandeliers, proclaiming with understated professional pride that all kinds of repairs would be 'neatly executed'. The business prospered and the firm later moved to Clarence Street and by 1937 was based in Camden Street. The company we know today however was reformed in 1947 by Basil Richardson who was joined some years later by Sisson Dalton and Gerard Gamble. Sisson Dalton took a very active role in the company for a number of years until his retirement in the late 1960s; it was Sisson Dalton who developed the catering supply side of the company which is still a feature of the business to this day. Until the early 1980s Gerard Gamble had been a sleeping partner for many years and is well known as the founder of Gerard Gamble Ltd also based in Leicester.

2, CANNING STREET,
Dr. to E. E. Smith,
PLUMBER, GAS AND BAR FITTER.
Gas Stoves Supplied and Repaired. All Kinds of Repairs Neatly Executed.

The company originally turned out pewter basins and brass fittings for beer pumps. The firm continued to make old style beer pumps until pressurised beer became common in the 1960s.

The real story of the modern company of EE Smith, however, is very much the story of Basil Richardson.

In 1937 Edward Elija Smith hired the 14 year old Basil Richardson to join the firm as an apprentice jack-of-all-trades and he was soon earning his money turning out pewter basins - still in use before the advent of stainless steel - and brass fittings for beer pumps. Two years later Hitler invaded Poland, war was declared and shortly afterwards the eighteen year old Basil volunteered for the armed forces.

Basil Richardson served in the Royal Navy from 1941 leaving with the rank of chief petty officer. Basil must have often spent time during those years pondering what his future and that of EE Smith's would be. On Basil Richardson's return from war service in 1947 the twenty-four year old found the now ageing EE Smith in failing health and the business rapidly running down. Astonishingly, despite being only twenty-four years old and having served only four years of his apprenticeship Basil agreed to take over the company and found himself as Managing Director , foreman and workforce! The firm was by then based in a small workshop in Mansfield Street. Who could have predicted whether or not the patient would survive. It is doubtful that many men would have been able to save a company already apparently on its deathbed let alone build it up to the massive undertaking it was to become. With an indomitable spirit and unflagging hard work Basil Richardson not only saved the company but put it back on the long road to prosperity, in the process creating secure, skilled jobs along with a reputation for getting a job done right, at the right price and of the best quality.

Top left: *Edward Elija Smith, founder of the company.*
Above: *An invoice dated 1898*
Right: *Basil Richardson, who joined the firm as a 14 year old apprentice and eventually took over the business following the second world war.*

Not surprisingly the dynamic management of Basil Richardson led to many changes after the period of wartime shortages of both men and materials. New ideas, new markets and increased efforts to expand the company's sales were the order of the day. No doubt many observers expected the returning sailor to be a failure but if so Basil Richardson soon confounded his critics. It was not to be too long before the company was expanding. In the late 1940s and early 1950s under Basil's inspired leadership extra craftsmen were soon being employed to make furniture, bars and fittings for pubs and hotels in addition to the regular output of metalwork and beer pumps.

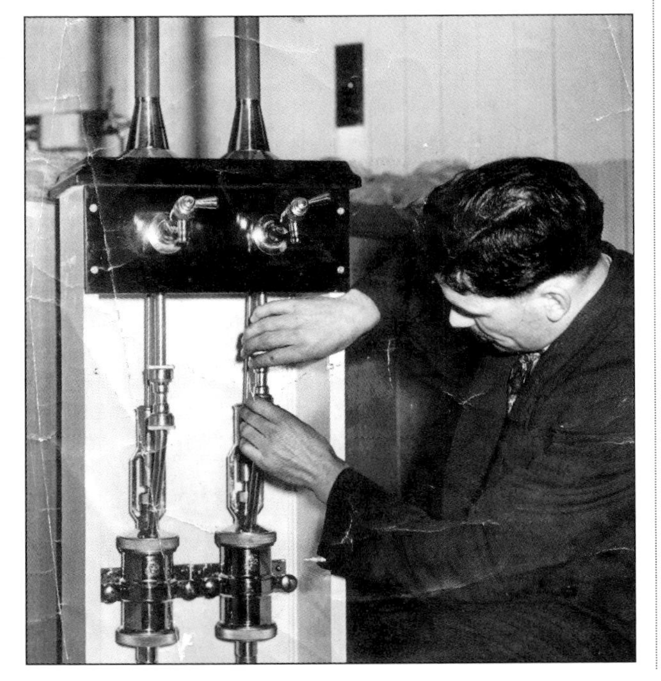

The company had relocated again this time to tiny premises in Waterloo Street opposite the Admiral Beaty public house, now long since demolished to make way for Waterloo Way. Also at this time a larger joiners shop was established in Shenton Street. After only a short stay in Waterloo Street the firm moved again this time to Byron Street before setting up permanent home in premises in the Clarendon Industrial estate. An indication of the firm's increasing prosperity was that these premises were purpose built by the company itself in 1966. That same year saw the company change its name from EE Smith Bar Fitters to EE Smith Contracts. Basil Richardson described the change as 'losing the pub image'.

The change of name signalled a wider range of services, particularly shop fitting. The firm's increasingly expert team were able to offer clients a complete service from specialised design and building through to complete interior fitting, providing furniture, upholstery and even choosing the glass and cutlery.

Left: *Basil Richardson adjusting a 'Coronation' beer engine, which he designed and manufactured himself.*
Below: *EE Smith's premises on Waterloo Street pictured in the early 1960s.*

Providing such a comprehensive service is a highly specialised business and EE Smith is deservedly recognised as one of the best in the country.

Basil Richardson's sons Rodney and Nigel are now Joint Managing Directors; since Basil's retirement in 1990 they continue to develop EE Smith Contracts Ltd. The brothers have established a new company Clarendon Fabrications Ltd a special work-surface manufacturer, and EE Smith Ltd property development company and they are continuing to expand the hire company started by Basil now known nationwide as 'Hire It All'.

The present directors recall that in the early days Basil did everything but as the company developed Sisson Dalton joined the company and developed the catering supplies side of EE Smith. As the company became more established Basil was also joined in the early days by Richard Onderka and Michael Abell who both later became directors.

Top: *The opening of the Strathallen Hotel, Birmingham in the early 1970s. It is an example of one of the firm's early interior fittings. Pictured from left to right are Sisson Dalton, George Montgomerie, Basil Richardson, George Anderson.*
Above left: *EE Smith Contracts circa 1975.*
Above: *An early themed pub 'The Viking', for which EE Smith Barfitters designed and fitted the interior decor.*

Today customers of the firm include most major hotel groups and many interior designers who specialise in high quality interior fitting out. Specialist joinery manufacture remains at the core of the business however, the firm also specialises in developing and expanding designers' concepts into a workable, completed, high quality product. A large percentage of the firm's work comes from Hotel interiors, new fittings out from concrete shell to completion, including design development, refurbishment, and re-fitting older properties. In recent years EE Smith has carried out refurbishments on cruise ships including the QE II, the Houses of Parliament and Windsor Castle.

The firm has carried out projects overseas, much of its turnover in the early nineties recession was from Germany and the firm has worked in most European countries since then - and even further afield including St Petersburg in Russia, Croatia and Malta.

EE Smith's greatest selling point is that the firm employs a whole spectrum of specialised trades and craftsmen in conjunction with state of the art production equipment; the company is therefore able to offer traditional inlaid veneer marquetry, French polishing etc. alongside CNC produced precision components combining to produce the highest quality products at competitive prices.

And the firm is taking care of the future: 'Craftsmanship and training are their technical superiority, they believe in training and each year continue to take school leavers from the age of sixteen, up to six youngsters a year, who after technical college and EE Smith's own in house training become some of Leicester's most highly skilled craftsmen'.
Many of the craftsmen working at EE Smith started their working lives as apprentices with the firm and the fact that so many stay and progress their careers within the company is a tribute to the firm's management style.

How does the firm view the future? The present management believes that by working together with their clients, as part of a team, enables them to jointly produce a better product and are always looking for ways to improve their service with the use of technology to augment their traditional skills. They are committed to developing the company and subsidiaries and consolidating the firm's position and reputation as a leader in interior contracting.

The company's motto 'Quality and service in partnership' are sentiments which would no doubt have been heartily endorsed by Edward Smith back in the early days of the business when he too sought to provide a quality service to the inhabitants of Victorian Leicester. Edward Elija Smith would have trouble recognising today's business but he would certainly recognise the aspirations which underpin it.

Top left: *An aerial view of Leicester in the mid 1960s. EE Smith Barfitters is the white two storey angular building above the large oval building on the lower right of the picture. The Abbey Motor Hotel is the smaller oval building under construction in the centre of the picture.*
Below: *Celtic Manor Hotel showing the view from the Atrium down into the Reception lounge.*

A firm built of more than just bricks and mortar

An interest in carpentry from an early age led to Arthur Cawrey's involvement with the building industry. He formed a successful building and development company which has operated in Leicestershire for over 50 years.

Arthur Cawrey was born on 8th April 1920 in the Charnwood Street area of Leicester. He spent his childhood days at the Gateway School near the centre of Leicester and it was there that his talent for woodwork first came to light. Whilst a student at the school, Arthur gained a Silver Medal in Building Technology. This qualification, in turn, led to his apprenticeship as a carpenter in a joinery shop. In 1940 he passed his final exam in Carpentry and Joinery in the first class, awarded by the City and Guilds of London Institute. It was not long before Arthur progressed in his career and became site foreman and, within a few years, a director with Calverley, a local building company which ceased trading in the late 1970s.

Despite holding a prominent position at Calverley, Arthur was an ambitious and enterprising man and in 1948 he made the decision to leave the company and set up in business on his own. Arthur formed a partnership with Fred Bowles and the new company was established as Cawrey-Bowles Limited. The firm began operating from offices in Hinckley Road, Leicester. After the war, housing was needed urgently and soon the firm was contracted to build housing estates for local authorities. The first major contract was undertaken for Market Bosworth Urban District Council. During the early years of the company, Arthur fulfilled a variety of roles including estimator, buyer and site manager, watching over the construction which was carried out using brick laid with lime mortar, produced in a mortar mill.

Top: *Arthur Cawrey. Portrait taken in 1967 in his role as President of the National Federation of Building Trades Employers Leicestershire Association.* **Above right:** *Arthur Cawrey's Certificate in Carpentry and Joinery awarded in 1940.* **Right:** *Arthur Cawrey's daughters, Jean and Mary, with the company offices in the background, formerly used as a milking shed. 1956.*

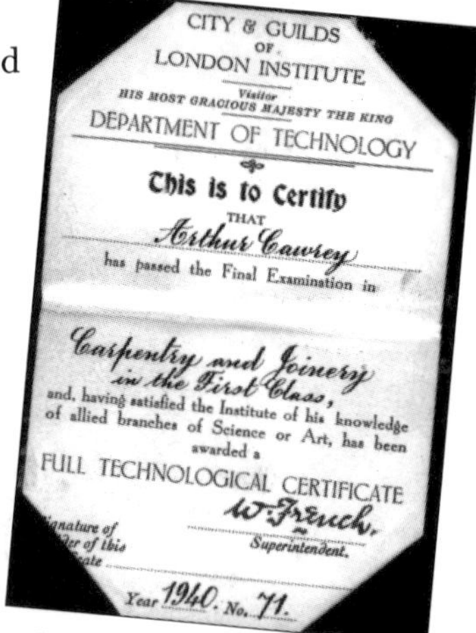

CITY & GUILDS OF LONDON INSTITUTE
Visitor
HIS MOST GRACIOUS MAJESTY THE KING
DEPARTMENT OF TECHNOLOGY
This is to Certify
THAT
Arthur Cawrey
has passed the Final Examination in
Carpentry and Joinery in the First Class,
and, having satisfied the Institute of his knowledge of allied branches of Science or Art, has been awarded a
FULL TECHNOLOGICAL CERTIFICATE
W. French, Superintendent.
Year 1940. No. 71.

In 1952 the partnership between Arthur and Fred Bowles came to an end and Arthur founded Cawrey Limited. Under the newly formed company, much of the work was general contracting. The new-build construction was mainly for local authority housing estates, but included some private houses and factories. During the mid 1950s the firm built its first school at Overdale Road in Wigston.

By 1954 the company had grown to such an extent that it was necessary to move to larger premises. Cawrey Limited moved into converted milking sheds at Gorse Hill, Anstey. It was also in this same year that the firm took on an apprentice, Michael Freeman, who started working as a bricklayer but progressed to become a site agent in 1974 and is still working for the company over 45 years later!

The year 1969 was a significant one for the firm. It was in this year that work started on building new houses in Ratby, a village five miles north-west of Leicester. Work on the development has gradually continued ever since with the company obtaining planing consent for new sections whenever the opportunity became available. In fact, by 1999 Cawrey Limited had built a total of 750 homes on this development as well as planting over 4,000 trees.

Throughout the 1970s the company's focus gradually switched to speculative housing and the firm continued to flourish. The 1980s opened with a happy event, when Arthur's son, John Cawrey, joined what could then be called the family firm.

By 1988, one of the company's long-term employees, Ken Callis who had been a director since the early 1960s and had taken over the duties of estimator, buyer and quantity surveyor, finally retired.

Sadly in 1990, Arthur Cawrey died after a short illness. The founder had remained Managing Director until his death and he was succeeded by his son, John, who took the company forward in his father's name. Under his leadership, in 1998, the company relocated to Kirby Grange Farm in Ratby and a year later could boast a turnover of £1.5 million and a permanent staff of 15.

***Top:** Early system building in Leicester. **Above:** John Cawrey, aged 6, on the trowel. **Above right:** A new four bedroomed house on a recent section of the Ratby development. **Right:** New three bedroomed house in Ratby.*

Today, Cawrey Limited continues to thrive. Most of the work undertaken consists of speculative housing development, however, some work is carried out for housing associations and Local Authorities and the company also has investments in commercial office and light industrial premises. After over 50 years of experience, Cawrey Limited has built its success on more than bricks and mortar. Indeed, it is this experience, combined with a flexible approach and the commitment of the company's long term staff that will ensure that Cawrey Limited's success continues in Leicestershire into the future.

Relishing the flavour of success

The origins of the Leicester based family firm, Driver's Pickle and Vinegar can be traced back to the year 1906. It was in this year that the company's enterprising founder, Frederick Charles Driver took the ambitious step of setting up his own business.

Frederick had spent the previous years of his working life gathering valuable experience as a wholesale grocer. Having sold pickles, Frederick realised that this was a lucrative trade and that there was a gap in the market ripe for him to fill. This he did and Drivers Pickle and Vinegar began in operation from premises in Grasmere Street (now known as Burnmoor Street). In the early days of the firm's history, the business was a one man concern with very basic equipment and the sour pickle and vinegar products were delivered with the use of a horse and cart.

The firm gradually developed and, although still a one man business, was stable enough to remain intact during the years of the first world war. It was in the inter-war period that Driver's Pickle and Vinegar first became a family firm. Frederick's son, John William Driver joined the business in the 1920s and generally lent a hand wherever it was needed. Sadly however, in 1933, Frederick Charles Driver died and John took over the running of the business.

Above left: *Company founder, Frederick Charles Driver.* ***Below:*** *The company's original premises.*

Unfortunately for John, he was not able to enjoy running a successful concern for long. His leadership was interrupted by the advent of the second world war. During the war John served in the airforce and consequently, the business was completely closed. The stock was disposed of, the vans were requisitioned and the factory was let to Swans, a hosiery firm that also operated from Grasmere Street.

It was not until the cessation of hostilities and John's demobilisation that the company was reformed once again. By that time the Drivers had moved to a house in Hazel Street and it was from works behind the house that Drivers Pickle and Vinegar re-opened. John, like his father before him, had to start from scratch as a one man business but, also like his father, John made a success of the firm and over the following years the business began to thrive.

Sadly, in 1955, John William Driver died. At the time John's son, Frederick Charles Driver who had grown up with the family firm, was undertaking his National Service. Frederick was faced with the decision either to see the business close again or leave his National Service after just two weeks and take over the running of the firm. Naturally, he chose to run the firm and took over in 1956.

Under Frederick's guidance, the firm expanded throughout the 1950s to cover the buildings from Hazel Street to Sawday Street. The first basic machinery was introduced during these years and in the early 1960s, the company was able to purchase a small van. By the 1970s the firm had grown and developed and onion peeling and other machines had been installed, increasing the company's productivity. The decade of the 1980s was one of further success. The firm's first computers were installed during this time and the company's fleet of lorries expanded. In fact, the density of traffic proved too much for the old premises and in 1987, Driver's Pickle and Vinegar moved to new, larger premises at Scudamore Road in Leicester.

In or around the year 1995, with the use of agencies, the company first began exporting its products. By then, Driver's Pickle and Vinegar also produced a wide range of products including relishes and sauces. As the export business developed these products were sold to countries such as, the USA, the Middle East and Malta.

Today, the company supplies over 64 different products and operates from an 18,000 square foot unit. The firm's main markets are national wholesale catering distributors covering MoD contracts, local authorities and hospitals as well as any catering food outlets. The company has grown considerably since its days as a one man operation and now employs 18 people. Yet another generation of Drivers has joined the family firm, Stuart Driver is in charge of Production and Quality Control, James Driver is in charge of Sales and Alan Driver is in charge of Buying Control. Indeed, with their help and a company motto that promotes the treatment of every customer to the best of your ability as small customers grow and large ones expand, Driver's Pickle and Vinegar will, no doubt, be able to relish the flavour of success for many more years to come.

Above: *A page from the company's ledger dated 1924.* ***Below:*** *A label for Driver's Pickled Onions.*

A company that is a credit to Leicester

The Mutual Clothing and Supply Company has been catering for the credit and retailing needs of the people of Leicester now for over a hundred years. Today, the company offers its extensive services from its 14 offices and 10 shops located all around the United Kingdom.

It was in the year 1898 that the company first began its life when the founder, Charles Edward Keene set up a business of his own. Charles Edward lived in Bradford and worked for Provident, a similar business to the one he was to found. However, when he made the ambitious and enterprising decision to start up on his own, he chose Leicester as the location in which to do this. Charles was a Methodist and had friends in the Methodist Movement in Leicester so, he moved from Bradford and founded what was to become, the Mutual Clothing and Supply Company Limited.

The fledgling firm began as a check trading concern. The firm issued a club check, like a credit card, this was accepted as cash by local retailers, the firm paid the shops and in turn, the customers paid the firm. Before the establishment of the business the weekly instalment trade was largely in the hands of the Packman, an individual trader who provided working men and women with the opportunity to buy decent clothes and furniture which they otherwise could not have had. However, Charles Edward's Mutual Shopping System offered more choice and lower prices and as a consequence, soon made the Packman an unnecessary feature in every day life.

The Mutual Clothing Club's head office was located at Pike Street, Wharf Street in Leicester and was open from 9 to 6.30 on weekdays and 9 to 1 on Saturday. This was then added to when one of the first shops was opened in Churchgate.

With these developments it was not long before the firm began to thrive and it even managed to continue trading throughout the first world war. Charles Edward's son, Charles Robert was also a Methodist and worked in the Red Cross during the war. After the cessation of hostilities Charles Robert joined his father's business as a general manager and he was joined, by his brother Walter. Charles Robert subsequently pursued a role as a politician to become Lord Mayor and he later had a local college named after him, the Charles Keene College.

In 1922, the family firm was incorporated as a limited company and became, Mutual Clothing and Supply Co Ltd, with Charles Edward as Governing Director and Charles

***Top left:** C Robert Keene. **Top right:** Chas E Keene. **Below:** Two of the early Mutual Shopping Guides.*

Robert as Managing Director. Throughout the 1920s, the firm expanded, recruiting agents and Walter opened new branches in Coventry and Nuneaton. The firm's premises were extended and a range of Kingstone Pianos as well as Gramophone, Record and Wireless departments were added to the store.

The 1930s was an eventful decade for the company. Further branches were opened in Leamington, Northampton and Oxford and the firm's current shop, Leicester's largest credit store, was opened on Belgrave Street. The shop was called Kingstone and offered modern showrooms and warehouses.

During the second world war several of the company's agents were called up, the Birmingham and Reading branches closed, the Kingstone store was requisitioned by the Ministry of Supply and the company could not charge interest but relied on voluntary payment. Despite this, Charles's son, Robert Charles rebuilt and expanded the company after the war and gradually took over from his father.

Under Robert's leadership more branches were opened in Peterborough, Corby and Norwich and then Nottingham. In 1974 the Consumer Credit Act was passed allowing companies to lend money. Consequently, over the following five years the business developed its money lending trade. This soon overtook the trading cheque business which was eventually replaced by gift vouchers. This successful development meant that during the 1970s and 1980s the company was able to open new branches in Derby, Mansfield and Wellingborough.

Today, with another branch opened in Doncaster, the Mutual Clothing Supply Company Limited continues to flourish with 14 offices, 10 shops and over 400 staff. Indeed, with the help of these loyal employees and the fourth generation of Keene's, Andrew Charles, now working for the family firm, Mutual Clothing Supply Co Ltd is still keen to impress and therefore, will continue to be a credit to Leicester for many years to come.

Top: *The new three storey Kingstone store under construction in the mid 1930s.* ***Above left:*** *The current Mutual Shopping Guide.*

A firm tailor-made to fit its window of opportunity

The Leicester based company, Barlow Blinds Limited supplies and manufactures internal window blinds and exterior awnings. The history of the company is a long and distinguished one that can be traced back to the year 1890.

It was in 1890 that the company's founder, Alexander Barlow took the bold and entrepreneurial decision to set up a business of his own. Alexander named his fledgling firm, E A Barlow and began manufacturing window blinds and awnings from premises in Leicester. In these, the early days, the blinds and awnings were put together using timber and canvas with a cotton base.

It was not long before Alexander's firm began to flourish. By 1927 E A Barlow was operating as a general window blind manufacturer, working from works called, The Excelsior, located at 202 and 204 Humberstone Road in Leicester. The firm advertised its services as including, 'Revolving Shutters Made and Repaired', 'Old Blinds Repaired and Re-Painted on the Shortest Notice', 'Roller Blinds with Patent Furniture'. The development of the firm to this successful stage had required a lot of hard work and dedication from Alexander and by 1927 he decided that it was time for him to retire from the business and pass it on into someone else's capable hands. Frank Herbert Coleman was the aforementioned capable successor of Alexander Barlow and he bought the company, its workshop and shop. In a letter announcing this change of ownership Frank stated, 'Mr E A Barlow feeling that he has earned a more restful time, has arranged that I shall carry on the business...Mr Barlow being good enough to still give me his valuable help in the practical work for part time'. So, with Alexander's advice and help, Frank took the reigns of the business and led it successfully forward.

In 1928, Frank's son, Alan Alfred Coleman joined the company aged just 17. He did not stay at the

Below: *Alan Coleman pictured with the motorcycle and sidecar purchased to make all the deliveries.*

existing premises very long however as, in 1931, the firm moved further along Humberstone Road to new premises situated at number 346. The 1930s were eventful times for Alan and in 1937 he married Peggy Sills who also joined the family business taking the number of employees up to five.

The advent of the second world war brought with it a temporary halt to the progress of the company. Alan Coleman was drafted into the army and the firm was closed. Sadly, during the war, Frank Herbert Coleman died. However, at the cessation of hostilities, his son took over the running of the firm which re-opened in 1946 from a garage at 57 Woodbridge Road. A motorcycle and side car was purchased to make all the deliveries.

In 1947 the company was able to move again, this time to 1,200 sq ft premises located at 73a Stanley Street. Indeed, it was from these premises, seven years later, that the firm produced its first bellow for Wadkin.

The 1960s proved to be a decade of expansion. Not only did the business move to larger, 3,000 sq ft premises at 110 Green Lane which were purchased for £2,500 but the staff levels increased to eight and, in 1962, the firm was incorporated as a limited company becoming, Barlow Blinds Limited. Also, in 1964 Brian Coleman, the company's present Managing Director joined the firm aged 21 on a wage of £16 per week!

In 1972 Alan Coleman died and Brian took over the running of the business. Under his leadership, in 1972 the factory was extended by 600 sq ft and a year later a blind shop situated at 54 Uppingham Road was leased at £2,000 per annum. The shop soon prospered and in 1978 it was purchased with the help of a bank loan for £18,000.

The rapid development of the previous two decades meant that by the 1980s the company was continuing to thrive. In 1981 the firm purchased its first computer, an 8K memory Amstrad. However, 1987 was probably one of the most successful years in the company's history. It was in this year that 40 retail outlets were added for Starlite Roller and Verts and a trade brochure for architects was produced. Blinds were advertised at £1,600 per month.

The modern blind is a sophisticated product with options for electric and automated control using sun and wind sensors.

Computerisation allows the company to offer customers drawings of their property with awnings added and all advertising, finance and product costs are controlled on the company's networked computer system.

Today, Barlow Blinds Limited continues to play an important role in Leicester. Although the materials have changed from the early days of the firm's history, now with aluminium, acrylic fabric and plastic components in use, the company's mission remains the same. Indeed, with the fourth generation of Coleman's, Phil Coleman, now involved in the family firm, Barlow Blinds is set to continue providing a quality, tailor made product and service, exceeding its customers expectations.

***Top:** Barlow's awnings outside a shop in the 1930s.*

A driving force in Leicester

The Leicester based bus operating company, Arriva Fox County is today part of the third largest bus group in the United Kingdom. However, this was not always the case, the company has gradually built up its leading position over more than 85 years in existence.

The origins of the company can be traced back to its connections with the British Electric Traction Company which operated tramways in Birmingham and the Black Country and in 1899 acquired a horse bus company. The Arriva Fox County Company was originally known as the Birmingham and Midland Omnibus Company and was established as a subsidiary of the British Electric Traction Company and registered on 26th November 1904. Despite this, the company did not begin operating motor bus services in the area until 1912.

By the 1920s the operations had expanded to reach Leicester due to the initiation of services from Nuneaton and Tamworth. During the early years the business adopted the fleet name 'Midland' which appeared on the buses but the passengers quickly adopted the name 'Midland Red' which, in fact, years later became the official company name.

In 1922 the company moved to its first base at premises at Frog Island with garage space for 30 buses. Three years later it was necessary to extend further to a 10 bus garage located in Welford Road and then again in 1927 to Southgates Garage which had a capacity of 90 and remains a major unit today.

The firm's ever increasing expansion continued in the 1930s. In 1937, after using a temporary garage for two years, the company moved to a new purpose-

Right: *A single-deck bus built by BMMO showing the characteristic name embossed on the radiator.* ***Below:*** *A late example of a BMMO built bus carrying the standard livery of the National Bus Company.*

built garage in Sandacre Street. It was also at this time that the firm began building many of its own buses at the works in Birmingham.

The advent of the second world war meant that for the first time in the firm's history it was unable to expand. Instead, services were reduced and the buses were used to evacuate schools and some were even converted into ambulances.

In 1946 production began once again and over 100 buses were built from developed designs and prototypes. The firm soon reached its pre-war rate of expansion and continued to flourish.

The next significant change in the history of the company was implemented in 1969. Since 1930 the bus industry had been subject to Acts of Parliament, defining the operating environment and structure of the business and 1969 was no exception. In this year the business was absorbed into the National Bus Company and this resulted in a change of livery to light red colours. Further local government reorganisation in 1974 brought rather less positive changes to Midland Red. Many services passed over to the newly created West Midlands Passenger Transport Executive and ultimately, this led to the division of Midland Red. In 1981 this division was cemented when Midland Red East Limited was created to service Leicestershire with garages in Southgate Street, Station Road in Wigston, Sandacre Street and Coalville and Swadlincote.

However, this was by no means the end of the story. In 1984 the company changed its name to Midland Fox Limited and successfully relaunched its services with a new red and yellow livery. Over the following three years the protection provided to services by Leicester City Transport was removed as were the strict licensing laws.

The lifting of these restrictions meant that Midland Fox was able to embark upon a major development of its services. Amongst these developments was the launch of a network of 97 Ford Transit minibuses in the city, completed in 1986.

However, the most important development was completed in 1987 when the Management Team acquired the business from the National Bus Company and then consolidated this success with the acquisition of a number of local companies including; Wreake Valley travel, County Travel and Astill and Jordan.

The late 1980s saw further acquisitions. In 1989 Drawlane Transport acquired Midland Fox which became British Bus and itself was acquired in 1996 by the Cowie Group which subsequently became one of the largest bus groups in the UK and changed its name accordingly to, Arriva. Under Arriva the company continued to go from strength to strength.

Today, the Arriva Fox County Company runs buses in Leicestershire from three depots and shares management with Arriva Derby. The company operates a very modern fleet with the latest low floor buses ensuring accessibility and convenience for everyone. With a fleet of 10,000 buses and operations in the Netherlands, Denmark and Spain combined with major car dealer outlets in the UK as well as Arriva Rental, the company is set to continue as a driving force in Leicester for many more years to come.

***Top right:** A bus timetable from the 1950s.* ***Above left:** All Arriva buses are being transformed with the aquamarine and stone livery.* ***Left:** In the mid 1980s major developments included the launch of Midland Fox, the Fox Cub minibuses and the opening of the new bus station.*

From rubber to radiation

The Browne Group is a Leicester based company with a world wide reputation; the firm specialises in the development, manufacture and supply of chemical indicator monitoring systems. Medical and surgical products by the group are equally well known around the globe.

The firm was founded in 1870 by the original Albert Browne and was incorporated as Albert Browne Ltd in 1908. Albert Browne had previously earned his living as an agent selling rubber thread but soon struck out on his own selling medical and surgical sundries. The firm operated from premises in Bowling Green Street in Leicester until 1908 when, following incorporation, the business moved to premises in Chancery Street.

On forming a limited company Albert Browne took his sons into the business, a business which would flourish over the following decades. The firm's catalogues from the 1920s and 1960s reveal an astonishingly wide range of surgical and medical equipment being manufactured and offered for sale by the company. One entire catalogue for example is devoted solely to 'Hospital Requirements in Rubber' despite its huge listing of over three hundred different rubber products ranging from air cushions to surgeons' aprons it remains a strong reminder of the company's origins.

The firm did not however restrict itself solely to rubber goods, more than two hundred other products were on sale to hospitals: everything from patient trolleys through to chairs, operating tables, walking frames and stretchers. The firm remained in the ownership of Albert Browne's successors for two generations until 1972 when the business was finally sold by the Browne family.

Today the group incorporates Albert Browne Ltd, Browne Health Care Ltd and Browne International Ltd and is based at Chancery House in Leicester's Hamilton Industrial Park in Waterside Road.

The company has changed beyond all recognition from Albert Browne's day yet some things remain unaltered. Today the Browne's catalogue is as diverse as ever offering hospitals and medical practitioners an extraordinary range of surgical dressings

Above: *Albert Browne, founder of the firm.* ***Right:*** *An operating theatre trolley which was featured in Albert Browne Ltd's catalogue from 1961.* ***Below:*** *A ward chair, which also appeared in the 1961 catalogue.*

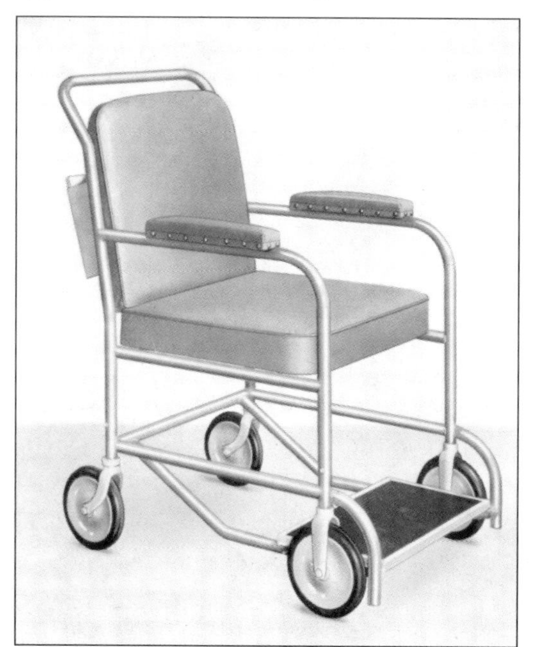

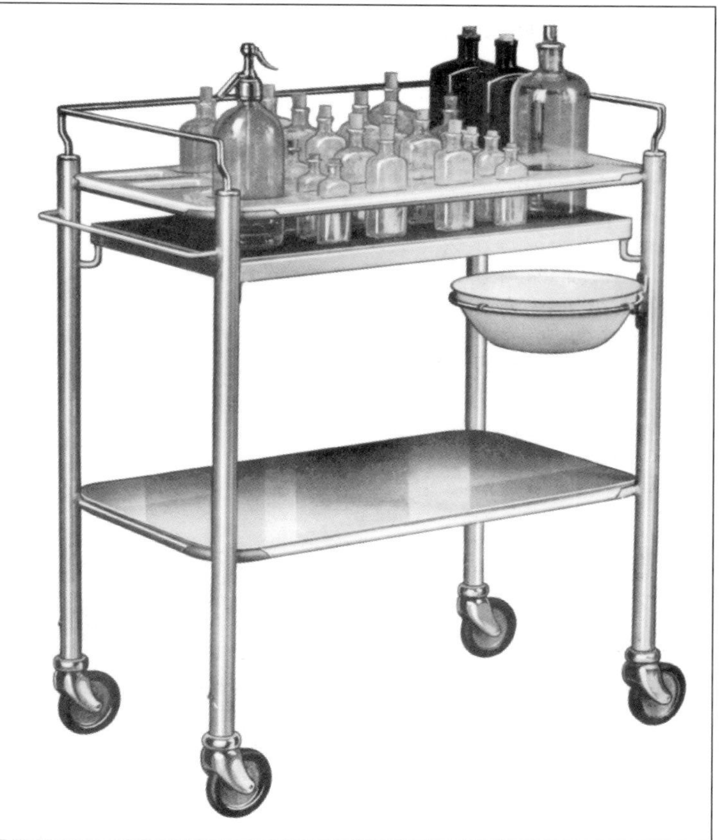

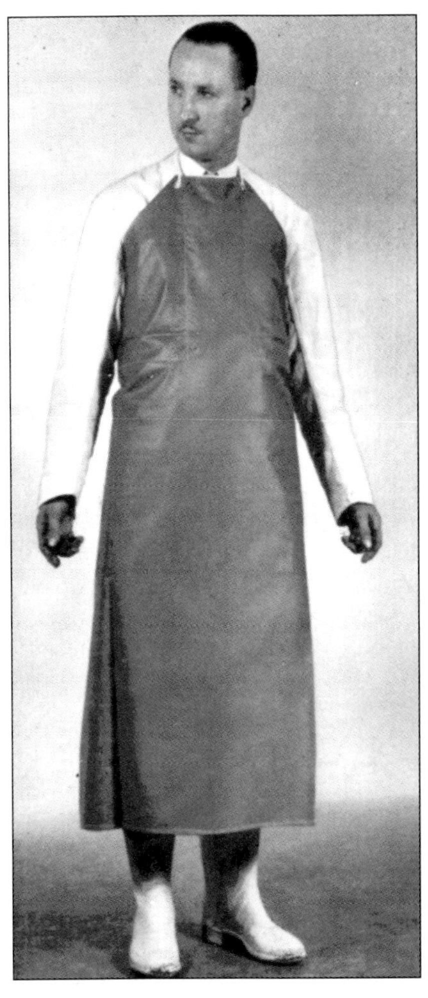

such as swabs and cotton wool, tourniquets and tongue depressors. Those reading the firm's catalogue for the first time will be astonished at the number of surgical scissors, forceps, tweezers and other instruments associated with the clinical professions.

Quite what Albert Browne would have made of the many of today's products can only be guessed at. Many of today's stock items had not even been dreamed of in his day but the catalogue now includes fibre optic ophthalmoscopes and otoscopes along with electrosurgical equipment and ECG machines. At least the firm's founder would still recognise such traditional items as weighing scales, doctors' bags and stethoscopes!

What Albert Browne would have undoubtedly found most surprising is the growth of the business as a developer, manufacturer and supplier of chemical indicators used in both hospital settings and in the food industry. The chemical indicators monitor the critical parameters necessary for successful sterilisation processes and are manufactured to perform in steam, ethylene oxide, formaldehyde and Gamma irradiation environments.

Incorporating Albert Browne Ltd, Browne Health Care Ltd and Browne International Ltd the Browne Group of companies is a world leader in the development, manufacture and supply of such chemical indicator monitoring systems. With expertise in medical pharmaceutical, veterinary and food technology-based industries the group specialises in chemical indicator technology for all commonly used sterilisation and disinfection processes.

Today Albert Browne Ltd is the manufacturing and research and development arm of the group. Purpose built research and development laboratories mean that A Browne Ltd stays at the forefront of chemical indicator innovation. Browne Health Care Ltd and Browne International Ltd are the sales and distribution arm of the group. Browne Health Care Ltd supplies hospitals, pharmaceutical companies and veterinary clinics with Browne products. Browne International Ltd supplies Browne's products to over 70 countries throughout Europe and the rest of the world through a network of agents and distributors penetrating markets as competitive as France and Germany, as far away as Australia and as different as China and Latvia.

That the Browne Group knows where it is going is made absolutely clear by the group's Mission Statement: 'To develop and position the business so that it is recognised world-wide as a principal producer and supplier of quality monitoring systems to the niche market in medical, food and related technology based industries whilst retaining its independence as a privately owned business'. Albert Browne would have been amazed to discover how far his small company would go.

Top left: *A surgeons apron from the 'Hospital Theatre and Ward Equipment' catalogue, 1961.* ***Below:*** *The head office at the end of the 20th century.*
Bottom: *Staff pictured outside the head office in 1999.*

Leicester on display

One of Leicester's best known companies is Antone Displays. The roots of the present business are to be found in the Northamptonshire village of Abthorpe close to Silverstone racing circuit.

The business began life as RG Displays in the early 1960s when it was owned and managed by the husband and wife team of Mr and Mrs Robert Gray.

In 1963, following Robert Grays early death, Mrs Gray sold the business to Wallin and Rowe Ltd letterpress and lithographic printers based in Copdale Road Leicester. The current owner and chairman Paul Ransom was asked to caretake the organisation at that time. During his initial involvement the company specialised in large black and white photographic prints mounted on hardboard panels. The facilities at that time included a small woodworking plant. To keep the workshops busy the company produced a multitude of product displays for Mettoy, Rest Assured and Dunlop car components. The firm eventually started to specialise in exhibition work. At this time the company was renamed Displays Ltd.

Two years later Wallin and Rowe was put up for sale and eventually purchased by the Oxley Press Group which reluctantly took on Displays Ltd. Things did not always go smoothly in those days, on one particular occasion the firm made an exhibition stand for Scott Bader for an International Exhibition. Unfortunately they discovered that it was so large they had to remove part of the roof to get it out of the workshops! On another occasion they made some beautiful displays for a toy fair for Palitoy but there was a near catastrophe when a temporary light bulb very nearly burned through a structural beam; fortunately it was spotted just in time and disaster was avoided.

In 1968 Oxley Press decided that Abthorpe was not the place from which to manage a significant subsidiary and brought the business to Archdale Street in Syston. At that time Oxley Press acquired Antone Display Studio, a Leicester-based silk-screen printing company and the two companies were combined, trading for the first time as Antone Displays Ltd. Tony Matts and Bill Hately were introduced as management; Peter Cooper with Tony Matts became joint managing directors. There were efforts made to integrate Antone Displays more into the Group's main activities when Ken Hatfield was introduced to the board, and cardboard engineering and a range of print finishing was added to the services on offer.

Antone Displays however never really settled happily into the Oxley Press group - but it did develop significantly in this period with exhibition and display work, screen printing together with cardboard engineering and print finishing. Palitoy, Scott Bader, Norprint and Norwich

***Top left:** Peter Cooper, joint Managing Director in the late 1960s.* ***Above right:** An aerial view of Antone Displays.* ***Right:** An instore stand for Estée Lauder, produced and installed by Antone Displays.*

Union were significant clients of the era and the construction side of the business was becoming the dominant force. In 1971 The company attracted the attention of the Regency Park Group, an advertising cum general marketing agency based in Nottingham. The Regency Park Group with its clients became very significant customers of Antone Displays and Oxley Press leapt at the opportunity to sell the company to them. This was not a happy period for Antone which was for a short period beset with financial problems until significant new business was introduced. Antone Displays was moved to new premises in Cross Street, Syston in 1972, which it still occupies.

The Regency Park Group soon got into difficulties and went into receivership though Antone survived through the good offices of the receiver, following which the firm was sold to Gomersall Jewellers in 1973. Tony Gomersall provided the company with the first period of stability in its history. Antone products were soon being used in the form of display counters the business eventually expanding to make Antone part of the Gomersall Display Group - which unfortunately later folded following some unwise acquisitions.

After the demise of the Gomersall Display Group Antone Displays was acquired by Paul Ransom who, in his own words, 'hocked everything to acquire the business'. After some early difficulties Antone eventually began to prosper concentrating on reliability and quality in its exhibition material and shop fixtures.

In 1986 Antone acquired the plant, equipment and staff of James & Beeby. When Des Beeby took the decision to stop trading. The firm initially rented his factory on Scudamore Road, Leicester but moved to the Syston premises the following year.

In 1987 there was a brief unhappy merger with Exporama followed by a rapid de-merger the legacy of which was a metal working department and an increased emphasis on shop fixtures.

By 1999 increasing business strength allowed the purchase of Key Display, another well -established Leicester business.

The present management of Antone Displays comprises Chairman Paul Ransom, David Gamble Managing Director, Mark Ransom running sales and marketing and Colin Parker in charge of production and Tony Wren, Finance Director.

Today Antone Displays is a one stop shop, employing more than 200 staff, where clients are offered a complete service from conception, to design, research, analysis, manufacture and installation using wood, metal, glass and plastics for a wide range of blue chip customers. Things have moved a long way from the days of RG Displays.

Above: *Chairman Paul Ransom and Managing Director David Gamble pictured outside the recently acquired premises of Key Displays.*
Below: *The Comet Group are another national company on Antone Display's client list.*

Planting the seeds of a Leicester firm and watching them grow!

The Leicester company James Coles and Sons (Nurseries) Limited was founded in 1914 by James Coles. Before founding his own nursery James had spent his working life gathering horticultural experience and knowledge.

In 1903 James moved to Leicester in order to manage James Wright's Nursery. After some years in this position he changed jobs and became the manager of Abbey Nurseries. Here James was joined by his brother, Bill, who was the Foreman and they worked together until 1913 when the lease expired.

James was an ambitious and resourceful man and wanted to set up his own nursery. He eventually accomplished this goal in 1914 when a chance meeting with a previous customer led to him finding an eight acre site in Evington. With £100 of his own money and a further £100 from a local charity James started James Coles and Sons Nurseries. A local firm gave him free credit for three years to pay for the stocks he purchased and with this help, it was not long before the nursery began to prosper.

In 1917 James was joined in the business by his sons, William (Bill) and Fred. The boys soon learnt about nursery crops and the company developed as a high class retail nursery supplying the large houses of Leicester.

A total of 16 acres were added to the nursery in 1926 and 1931 and, to cope with the expansion, Jim Fisk was hired as a propagator and assisted by Graham Adcock. In 1933, the firm purchased a shop in Leicester which was managed by Fred and sold bulbs and seeds. Bill on the other hand, assumed control of the newly established landscaping operation.

During the second world war the nursery was only allowed to continue to grow apple trees as food crops and inter plant with crops such as

***Left:** James Coles, the firms founder. **Right:** Bill Coles. **Below:** The retail plant centre at Thurnby.*

carrots, lettuce and onions. However, at the cessation of hostilities, the nursery resumed its path of expansion, concentrating on the wholesale market. In 1946 James retired and left his sons to run the business. Fred and Bill bought 25 acres of land and planted it with trees and due to the development of the glass and frame area started supplying stocks to public bodies as well as the existing retail customers.

In 1970, Bill purchased a 15 acre site at Barkby and rented a one acre propagation area nearby. This was added to in 1972 with the purchase of Anglings Farm at Gaddesby. It was also in this year that Bill's son Geoffrey, who had bought Fred's share of the company, signed a deed of partnership with his father and one of the nurseries long term workers Stephen Haines.

In 1978 the firm had grown to such an extent that it was able to be incorporated as a limited company and under the leadership of the two directors, Steve and Geoff, went from strength to strength. More land was purchased at Queniborough and Gaddesby and shrub production was started.

Throughout the 1980s and 1990s the trend for expansion continued with purchases at Stoughton, Gaddesby, Syston and Barsby taking the amount of land owned by the firm to over 400 acres. In 1987, after 70 years service, Bill retired after receiving the Pearson Memorial Medal for conspicuous services to the trade. Steve Haines retired in 1992 and was replaced by Tom Richardson and Geoff's son, James Coles.

In 1998 the landscape department was rewarded for all its hard work when one of its projects, a garden in Knighton was given the Principal Award in the BALI National Landscape Awards. A year later the company won two other awards, this time from the APL. Over the years the business has also received a total of three Royal Horticultural Society medals for various show gardens and two BBC Haymarket Awards for the Best in Show at the Gardeners World Live Exhibition.

Today the rapid growth and development of the company continues. The family firm is now one of Britain's largest growers of high quality trees, shrubs, climbers, roses and hardy herbaceous stock and with a ground capacity of two million plants, also produces one of the largest ranges. The company has an award winning landscape department that continues to carry out large scale projects throughout the Midlands and the stock is promptly distributed throughout the country with the use of the firm's own fleet of Scania lorries. Indeed at its foundation, James Coles planted the seeds of a successful company and subsequent generations are still seeing the fruits of his labour as James Coles and Sons (Nurseries) Ltd continues to grow.

Pictured above: *Just a small selection of the countless varieties of plants grown by the nursery.*
Below: *One of James Coles & Sons fleet of delivery lorries.*

A school with a distinguished past offering pupils a promising future

The Leicester High School for Girls is an independent school taking pupils between the ages of 3 to 18. However, this was not always the case. Indeed, the school has come a long way since its foundation in 1906.

It was in this year that Mrs Holles formed a kindergarten class for one girl and two boys in the schoolroom of Stoneygate Baptist Church. The school was named Merton House and established as a 'model school' for boys and girls. Gradually, the fledgling school grew and in 1925 Mrs Holles moved her pupils to new premises at Portland House, off London Road on the southern edge of Leicester. The Portland House building dates back to the pre-Victorian era and was, in fact, originally built in 1826 as a hunting lodge for the Duke of Portland. It has also been a coach house and a vinery.

From its new premises the school was renamed Portland House School and was soon recognised as a preparatory school by the Board of Education. During these, the early days of the school's existence, not only did the pupils dress in the distinctive yellow and grey

Top: *Portland House at the end of the 19th century.*
Below: *The magnificent library.*

striped blazers now synonymous with the school, but boaters and white gloves were also part of the uniform. Indeed, one teacher, new to the school, remembers being reprimanded for returning from the hockey field with the senior girls "improperly dressed" and so, the following week returned from the same hockey field with the same girls, covered in mud but wearing the regulation boaters and gloves!

The school's founder, Mrs Holles, retired in 1935 and Miss Mackirdy and Miss Alcraft took over the Headship. Miss Mackirdy retired in 1945 but Miss Alcraft carried on as Headmistress until her death in 1972. By 1945, things were beginning to develop and this year was also marked by the decision to pay staff on the Burnham Scale in order to attract teachers of an appropriate quality and standard.

In 1952, the school underwent its first full inspection by the Ministry of Education. This review lasted for a total of three and a half days and resulted in the conclusion that Portland House was to be recognised as a grammar school.

The school continued to thrive over the following 20 years, and the decade of the 1970s proved to be an eventful one. In 1972, Miss Alcraft's Deputy, Miss Day Storey, became the new Headmistress and it was also in this year that the subject of Chemistry was added to the curriculum. By 1975, the school had a total of 250 girls. This year was also important in that the school was constituted as a Charitable Trust and as such, administered and managed by a Board of Governors under the Chairmanship of the Bishop of Leicester. In 1976, adding to the expanded science curriculum, a

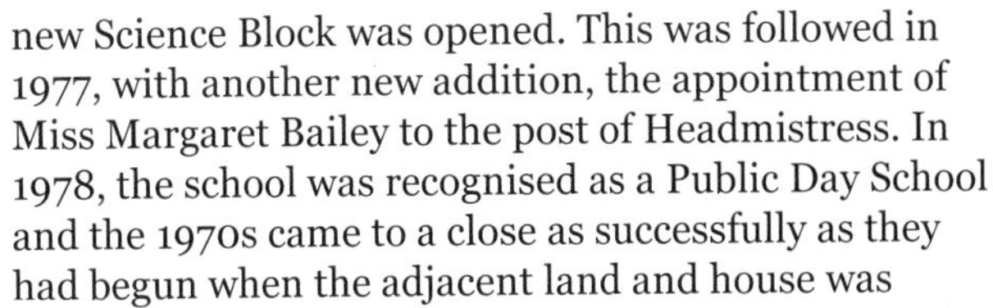

new Science Block was opened. This was followed in 1977, with another new addition, the appointment of Miss Margaret Bailey to the post of Headmistress. In 1978, the school was recognised as a Public Day School and the 1970s came to a close as successfully as they had begun when the adjacent land and house was purchased and converted into a Junior Department. The new Junior Department had its own detached house and play garden. This was soon added to, with a Kindergarten Unit and Preparatory classes.

In 1982, Mrs Dorothy Buchan was appointed Headmistress and three years later the school changed its name from Portland House to Leicester High School for Girls, the name it still goes by today.

In 1989, under its new name, the school was further extended with a new development - the provision of a gymnasium. In 1991 the Junior School, too, underwent a change of name to, Leicester High School for Girls Junior Department and a year later Mrs Patricia Watson took over the role of Headmistress.

The opening of a new millennium in the year 2000 was marked by the completion of a new library, a resources and careers area, a new laboratory, updated IT facilities and new music and drama rooms. These extensive developments were put into good use following an opening ceremony attended by HRH The Duchess of Gloucester.

Today, Leicester High School for Girls still reaches high academic standards and provides a fostering environment for its pupils. Indeed, the School continues to build upon its distinguished past and traditions in order to offer its pupils a promising future.

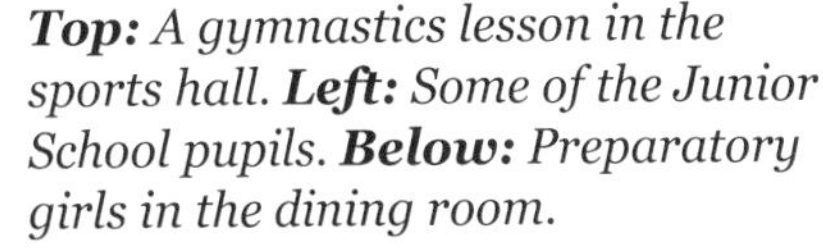

***Top:** A gymnastics lesson in the sports hall. **Left:** Some of the Junior School pupils. **Below:** Preparatory girls in the dining room.*

Leicester Tiger that's a roaring success

In an age where tradition, continuity, craftsmanship and care are increasingly rare, it is reassuring to come across a family business like Everards, Leicester's leading local brewery for over 150 years. Now based at Narborough, they are one of just over thirty regional breweries in Britain that still remain under family control.

William Everard, a farmer from Narborough, founded the business in Southgate Street at the heart of the city in 1849, having noted that England was rapidly changing and that the new industrialised society offered opportunities for a progressive approach to brewing. Since then, discerning beer drinkers in Leicester and beyond have enjoyed many millions of pints of the company's cask-conditioned ales. The two best known products being Tiger Best Bitter, named after the local regiment and Beacon Bitter, named after the highest landmark in the county.

Whilst the Everard family approach to brewing is steeped in tradition they have always emulated the vision of their founder and moved with the times. This may be the reason why the company has not only survived but thrived and been passed down across five generations, each time as a bigger and more successful business. The present Chairman Richard Everard, is William Everard's great, great grandson and has already declared his intent to maintain this custom.

From its early days, brewing and supplying local hostelries, the company grew to purchase its own pubs. Many of the earliest acquisitions remain in the Everards estate, which today comprises over 150 pubs of all types and sizes and which are located across Leicestershire and seven surrounding counties.

Drinking habits tend to reflect the changing fortunes of the economy and social change, so world wars, the 1930s depression, new leisure habits and rising drink taxation have all conspired to impede Everards' progress and to make continued growth both difficult and challenging.

However, William Everard established a culture when he founded the business with the simple adage that 'no effort should be found wanting in the production and supply of genuine ale of first-rate quality'. By remaining true his ideal and keeping a careful eye on the quality of Tiger and the other ales in their portfolio Everards have always attracted a loyal following. Their commitment to quality has paid dividends in other ways too, with many awards for product excellence being collected over the years.

Every glass of Everards ale contains more than just English hops, yeast and barley, it includes a long and interesting history centred upon the city of its birth.

***Top left:** Brewery founder, William Everard.*
***Below:** The King William IV in Earl Shilton, in the early days of the 20th century.* ***Bottom:** Southgate Brewery, circa 1875.*

Opening doors of opportunity

For more than 100 years, De Montfort University has been passing on knowledge and expertise, and opening the doors of opportunity to countless young men and women.

When a small School of Art was opened in Pocklingtons Walk back in 1879, the founders had no way of knowing that the institution they had established was destined to become the fastest growing university in Western Europe, and that by the end of the 20th century, it would be the largest distributed university in the United Kingdom.

Those original art classes targeted the textile and footwear industry, which were so much a part of Leicester, passing on skills that would provide employment to many students in and around the Leicester area. Swift expansion meant that by 1876 a move was called for, and with a total of 321 students the college removed to Hastings Street. Technical classes were later added to the syllabus, held in the Ellis Memorial Wing of the Wyggeston Boys School. An amazing range of courses was on offer, from paper hanging and the manufacture of boots and shoes to applied mechanics and electric light and power distribution.

By the end of the 19th century, £25,000 had been raised for the construction of a prestigious, purpose-built college, later to be named the Hawthorn Building. The School of Art and the Technical School joined forces and printed a joint prospectus, and the Bishop of London declared the new college building officially open on 5th October 1897. At that time the Technical School had 1,000 students and the School of Art 500.

The college continued to build on the natural abilities of its students, encouraging invention and innovation, training craftspeople to the very highest standard they were capable of achieving. Further expansion led in 1927 to the building of a new west wing, the Leicester colleges of Art and Technology. The Arts and Crafts syllabus included classes in Architecture, Draughtsmanship and, interestingly, Women's Crafts, while the College of Technology offered courses in Mathematics, Commerce, Electrical and Mechanical Engineering, Languages, Pharmacy and Biology, to name only a few.

The year 1969 was a key one in the development of the college: on 1st April the new City of Leicester Polytechnic was created, providing postgraduate, degree, diploma, and similar levels of higher education. A further stride forward was achieved in 1992, when the Polytechnic became De Montfort University.

The fastest growing university in Western Europe today has arms that reach into virtually every corner of the world, with a Business School in South Africa, an MBA programme in Jakarta, Art and Design in Penang and Business and Engineering in Kuala Lumpur, and research laboratories and partnership links in many countries. To quote the Vice Chancellor Professor Kenneth Barker CBE in 1997, 'It has reached the point where you might almost say that the only place left to go is outer space.'

Top right: *University students outside the main building.* ***Left:*** *The Queens building.*

Crispin Adhesives - giving the opposition some stick

A garage in Rolleston Road, Leicester, was the unlikely premises chosen by Jack Smalley when he set up the Crispin Chemical Company back in 1936. To those 'in the know', a clue to the purpose of the company lay in the name - St Crispin is the patron saint of leather workers. With the help of his wife (who looked after the firm's finances) and one other worker, Jack Smalley supplied leather softeners, finishes and adhesives to the traditional shoe trade in Leicester and Northampton.

Though the shadow of war already hung heavy over the country, the fledgling firm nevertheless grew and prospered, and after a few years moved to Coleman Road, which along with a second building acquired in Robinson Road, remain the company's premises today. Though the footwear industry provided the original outlet for Crispin Adhesives, as they became, by the beginning of the new millennium the business spanned some 20 different industries across the entire United Kingdom.

Since those early years, an extensive and diverse range of adhesives has been added to the company's products, which today fall into three main categories: water based Aquebond, Crisbond (hot melts), and Solibond, a solvent based adhesive. The Clearpaq brand was especially developed for plastics packaging. Though today's main markets are mainly in the areas of packaging, labelling and the food industry, Crispin adhesives turn up in many unexpected places including fireworks, snooker cues, billard tables, food labels - and amazingly, policemans helmets.

John Hall, Crispin Adhesives' Operations Director, puts the technical versatility of the company down to the expertise of his highly qualified and experienced workforce. It is in the company's on-site laboratory that academic and technical knowledge combine with many years of experience. Working under Development Director, Alan Herringshaw, Crispin Adhesives' chemists can formulate adhesives to meet almost any application.

It is the company's dedication to customer service and care, however, and the team's commitment to each customer's individual requirements, that have combined to establish Crispin Adhesives reputation for excellence. Official recognition added the icing to the cake when they received a Technology Fast 50 award from accountants Deloitte & Touche - and of course when Crispin Adhesives achieved accreditation to ISO:9001 in 1997.

As for the future, Crispin Adhesives are exploring new and diverse markets with a view to expansion and development of new products within the international arena.

Top left: *Company founder Mr Jack Smalley.* ***Above:*** *A poster advertising Crispin shoe adhesives from the 1940s.* ***Below left:*** *The firm's Leicester premises.* ***Below right:*** *The Technology Fast Forward award presented to the firm in 1999.*

The spark that took a Leicester company ahead of the flock!

The Leicester based company, Hiva Products has operated as one of the leading firms in its field for over three decades. Indeed today, Hiva Products has become Britain's leading flocking company. However, this leading position in the market place is not coincidental, but rather, has been worked for and built up ever since the company's original conception.

The firm was established on the 15th March 1955 by its founder, Thomas Patrick Woodcock (Patrick). Before taking the enterprising and ambitious decision to set up a business of his own, Patrick had spent his time wisely, gathering valuable experience whilst working as an electronics engineer. It was perhaps inevitable then, that when Patrick decided to take his skills and experience and transfer them to a company of his own, he would choose to establish an electronic engineering firm.

Patrick's company began its existence from premises located at Narborough Road in Leicester. Indeed, it was from this site that Patrick started to build his fledgling business as a manufacturer of High Voltage Generators. Due to the nature of the work, Patrick named his company, High Voltage Applications and under this name, from the outset, the firm began to flourish.

High Voltage Applications was a family firm from the start and Patrick was assisted by his sons, Tom and Peter. Together, the Woodcock family watched their business grow and in 1960 the extent of the expansion meant that the company could make its first move of many to new premises at Blaby. This move was followed in subsequent years by expansions to premises at Huncote, Cosby and Aylestone.

Gradually, the nature of the business moved into electrostatic flocking. In this process a base material is coated with an adhesive, millions of flock fibres are charged with a high voltage and applied to the adhesive surface to form a dense coating giving the material a fabric-like texture with a luxurious feel.

Today, Hiva Products produce packaging materials, cosmetics, jewellery, motif and garment decoration. The company offers an unrivalled range of materials to suit all types of applications from shoe fabrics to powder puffs. The third generation of Woodcocks now works for the family firm. Indeed, with their help the spark that took Hiva Products ahead of the flock will, no doubt, remain ignited for many more years to come.

Above: *Company founder Patrick Woodcock and his wife Kathleen.* ***Below:*** *The Cosby factory.*

A 1920s view of Leicester city centre with the clock tower as a focal point

Acknowledgments

Leicestershire Museums, Arts & Records Service

Leicestershire Records Office

Ken Wheatley

Thanks are also due to Ann Ramsdale for penning the editorial text and Steve Ainsworth for his copywriting skills